At Your Service

Also by Desmond Atholl & Michael Cherkinian:
That Girl and Phil

At Your Service

MEMOIRS OF A MAJORDOMO

Desmond Atholl
&
Michael Cherkinian

St. Martin's Press
New York

Design by Judy Christensen

Library of Congress Cataloging-in-Publication Data
Atholl, Desmond.
　　　At your service : memoirs of a Major
Domo / Desmond Atholl and Michael Cherkinian.
　　　　　　p.　cm.
　　　"A Thomas Dunne book."
　　　ISBN 0-312-08137-5
　　　　1. Atholl, Desmond.　2. Butlers—En-
gland—Biography.
　　　I. Cherkinian, Michael.　II. Title.
　　　TX334.1.A84A3　1992
　　　640'.46'092—dc20　　　　　　　92-25839
　　　[B]　　　　　　　　　　　　　CIP

First Edition: November 1992

10 9 8 7 6 5 4 3 2

To Nansy,
who inspired me to live the dream

Author's Note

Certain names, descriptions, and dates have been altered to protect the privacy of those individuals who have never willingly ventured into the blinding spotlight of public scrutiny. The experiences, impressions, and anecdotes I relate remain substantially intact.

ACKNOWLEDGMENTS

The authors would like to express their gratitude to the following individuals for their assistance: Reagan Arthur, Doris Borowsky-Straus, Harry Cherkinian, Nigel Dempster (and The London Daily Mail), Frank DiGiacomo, Donal and Mila Donnelly, Tom Dunne, Benno Friedman, Gideon Garthner, Lyn Goldberg, Andrea Hicks, Tim James, Norman Kurz, Toni Lopopolo, Barbara Lowenstein, Claudia Riemer, Maria Russo, Kim Sergio, Reed Sparling, Vera Louise Storey, and Nancy Yost.

Ad•ven•ture, 1. an undertaking of uncertain outcome; a hazardous enterprise 2. an exciting or very unusual experience 3. participation in exciting undertakings or enterprises 4. a commercial or financial speculation of any kind; venture 5. *Obs. a.* peril; danger; risk *b.* change; fortune; luck 6. to risk or hazard 7. to take the chance of; dare.

Prologue

Who could have possibly foreseen that a simple child's game would irrevocably alter the course of my life?; that it would unlock a Pandora's box of exotic locales, perilous situations, and strange and wild creatures whose only link was the technical name of their species: "Employer." I would eventually exchange my fellow game-player/sister for Arab and Indian princes, European royalty, Hollywood stars, disco divas, and that strangely misshapen yet powerful beast which arose out of the ashes of the self-indulgent seventies to light the financial fires of the excessively extravagant eighties: The Corporate Raider.

Instead of enacting the game within the confines of my grandparents' English home, the playing area would expand to include villas, castles, yachts, country estates, private jets, penthouse apartments, and a desert tent. My odyssey would eventually take me to such diverse cities as Paris, Nice, Rome, London, Naples, New York, Athens, Tehran, 'Aqaba, Abu Dhabi, Beirut, Bangkok,

Hong Kong, Zurich, Geneva, and that financial exclamation point of the universe: Beverly Hills. If Alice's adventures in Wonderland began by stepping through a mirror, then my adventures in servitude commenced by becoming a majordomo.*

From the beginning it was evident that I made remarkably unusual choices in everything I did: While most of my childhood contemporaries preferred such conventional play-acting games as "Cops and Robbers" or "Cowboys and Indians," I favored a fantasy of my own creation: "Mistress & Majordomo."

The game originated when I was seven; my sister Sarah—two years younger and two inches taller—became my playmate in crime. We conspired to "spy" on our grandmother and the household staff. Our mission: observe and duplicate their behavior down to the most infinitesimal detail. Sarah and I began to analyze our grandmother's voice reviewing menu choices for the day; we discovered that it was question-like, swirling upward in pitch—as if she were looking for an official confirmation. Charlotte (our cook and household manageress) would either (a) disapprove of the suggestion by scrunching her nose, cheeks, and mouth in what I presumed was her imitation of a prune, or (b) applaud the choice by bobbing her head and joyously exclaiming, "Oh, yes in-

---

*According to Webster's, the term *majordomo* is of Spanish and Italian origin dating back to 1589. Translated to "chief of the house," it describes the highest managing official of an important household, who is almost a domestic minister of state. The term is often used interchangeably in today's society with the word "butler."

xii

deed, Mum! One of the Master's favorite's! A very good choice indeed!" Charlotte's enthusiasm for the proper menu choice could equal the most evangelical of preachers in a room full of sinners.

From the inception of our game I was determined to play the role of the majordomo—*not* the mistress (or master, as the case may be). The majordomo appeared to be the more amusing role, scurrying from room to room performing duties—far more entertaining than the mistress' task of making various requests and then retiring to her library or ladies' clubs. My casting decision suited Sarah quite nicely who, from an early age, displayed a natural talent for placing orders. Sarah and I practiced for hours trying to refine our game. We had not set out as mere amateurs, but felt our accomplishments were worthy of a command performance for no less than Her Majesty, the Queen.

When Sarah was six she decided to have a formal dinner party to celebrate the first birthday of Evelyn, a beautiful porcelain doll which our mother had purchased for her in Thailand. She set about instructing me as to the type of china, silver, glassware, and tablecloths which were to be used for the very special occasion.

While my grandmother and Charlotte were "otherwise engaged," I quietly but diligently raided the butler's pantry. After gathering the necessary items, I proceeded to set the Hepplewhite table in the formal dining-room for our twenty-five make-believe guests. In an effort to achieve absolute perfection I carefully measured the distance between the place settings, finger bowls, glasses, and chairs. Many years later I would be able to glance at a table and instantly ascertain if a fork or spoon was a quarter inch too far to the left. Such a small variation may not matter to everyone, but creating a perfect table setting is an art form in which a professional majordomo takes great pride.

After I had determined that the table setting was flawless, I placed a selection of my favorite stuffed animals and Sarah's invited dolls in each of the chairs. While I began to assemble the centerpiece (an inspiration of cornflowers surrounded by seashells which I would duplicate fifteen years later for an Arab prince), my grandmother and Charlotte swept into the room; upon seeing the results of my hard work they froze in their tracks. Two heads, in perfect unison, darted back and forth between myself and the table. It looked as if they were watching the match-winning point of a tennis tournament. Certain that they were going to chastise me, I began to utter a feeble explanation. Much to my surprise, however, two of my favorite women in the world began laughing and patting me on the back for a job well done. From then on, my grandmother and Charlotte joined Sarah and myself in some of our make-believe dinner parties.

As I grew older I was surprised to learn that certain individuals might be willing to pay me to play the game which had been such a delight; for many years the profession I playacted my way into proved to be tremendously satisfying. When I moved to New York in 1982 my outlook began to shift: I was becoming less enthusiastic about my work. Occasionally (based on the particular employer at the time and his or her particular mood for the day) my job would remind me of the childhood game

I had so enjoyed with my sister. But after almost two decades of domestic employment I was losing the battle. The adventure was going out of it; something had changed. I realized that the players were operating with a new set of rules wherein all participants were no longer created equal. This primarily held true with certain American employers who did not hold domestic employees in the same regard as their European counterparts.

In retrospect, I believe the most important characteristic which Sarah and I learned to duplicate was the mutual respect and admiration between my grandparents and their household staff. And it was exactly this lack of respect between employer and employee which had so drastically altered my perspective on my profession.

After almost thirty years of playing the game I had loved so well, I decided to stop serving and start talking.

One

Growing up amongst the upper classes of British society is like attending a formal dinner party that never ends. It's a lovely place to visit, but living there can be a strain to even the most well-bred individual. Every event of the day—from breakfast to bedtime—has a precise list of rules and regulations; little is left to chance. When I was three my nanny diligently drilled me on the correct method for eating asparagus. She made it quite clear that if I did not properly execute the task I risked banishment from all worthy social functions, which would definitely have a detrimental effect on my life. Bearing that in mind, I tried to raise the steaming green stalk as carefully as a brain surgeon might lift his scalpel. Balancing it between my thumb and index finger, I envisioned my entire future hinging on a vegetable. Anyone who has not had the privilege of being raised in a formal environment might find it a bit oppressive. I was fortunate, however: I mastered the art of asparagus eating and developed a taste for formal dinner parties at a very early age.

The British aristocracy's approach to child-rearing is riddled with peculiarities. I'm certain the average American would find a mixture of nannies, nurses, tutors, and governesses overwhelming; such an assemblage of "substitute parents" may seem impersonal. But for an English family characterized by old money, elegant surroundings, formality, discipline, and impeccable manners, relying upon an entourage of support staff to raise one's child is considered quite sensible.

When I moved to America in 1980 and recounted the tales of my youth I was, understandably, mystified by some of the reactions I received:

"It must have been incredibly lonely for you."

"I don't think people should be allowed to have children if they aren't going to invest the time to raise them!"

"You probably spent a fortune on therapy trying to work through the anger of being abandoned by your parents."

Up until then, I had no idea I had survived such a troubled childhood. I was under the apparently mistaken impression that my early years had been a wonderfully happy experience. In order to gain the proper perspective on my adolescence, however, one has to realize that I was raised in a manner appropriate for my particular family within the British class system.

On a typical day I would not see my mother until precisely 4:00 P.M. Tea time: that sane and civilized hour when one pauses for a moment before continuing with the rush of the day's activities. Appropriately dressed in a jacket, tie, and short pants, I would be ushered by Nanny into a room which held faint traces of stale cigar smoke mixed with the flowery fragrance of an expensive

2

perfume. While seated upon a brown leather Chesterfield my mother and I shared Earl Grey tea, cucumber sandwiches, and polite conversation. After approximately twenty minutes, Nanny would escort me back to my room. Children usually take all of their meals in the nursery until they are at least five. The only other opportunity I had to visit with my mother or father was when they kissed me goodnight. I never questioned this particular arrangement or felt deprived of my parents' company; I understood it to be the proper way in which children interacted with members of their family.

The thought of sending a six-year-old to boarding school probably sends chills through the spines of America's most loving parents. But the English are not so sentimental; they have a strict attitude toward education. Amongst the aristocracy it is not only considered normal but absolutely vital to send one's child to a well-qualified preparatory school as soon as possible; the school's ability to educate the child is, in most instances, a greater consideration than its location. The idea of sending a youngster away is rarely regarded as an act of parental abandonment. There are schools in Europe which take toddlers as young as two. This contrasts greatly with the average American family wherein most children remain in the home until they are eighteen. In my case, however, it was not considered unusual when, at the age of six, I began my journey into the English school system.

Since my grandparents' estate was located two miles from the boarding school, and my father was a diplomat who traveled constantly, I spent most weekends with my maternal grandparents. Growing up in an environment colored by the mix of a strict Victorian Englishman and an eccentric but fun-loving ex-actress influenced the approach I would take to both my personal and professional lives: I learned to combine an appreciation for organization and discipline with a sense of fun and adventure. My work attitude is one of the characteristics former employers have most enjoyed. I not only ran a well-organized household, but also appeared to be having a tremendous amount of fun. A sense of humor, vitality, and a creative approach to one's job can affect even the most straight-laced and difficult of employers.

When I was working for an Arab Prince we traveled to Whadi Rumm (a desert near 'Aqaba in Jordan) with a small group for a mansef (a traditional desert feast consisting of lamb roasted on a spit served with yogurt and unleavened bread). A team of workers went ahead to set-up palatial tents complete with cooking areas, bedrooms, showers, and toilet facilities. Two hours before the feast was scheduled to begin, one of the young cooks approached me in a panic. Apparently after the kitchen had been organized the workers decided to take a break; they left the storage tent unattended. During their absence a pack of wild desert dogs decided to have their own private mansef: They ran off with two sides of lamb. The cooks didn't know what to do and were terrified to incur the Prince's wrath. Thinking quickly, I dispatched a trusted aide in a jeep to retrieve more meat from a nearby Bedouin encampment.

The gentleman arrived one hour later with more lamb but the meal was obviously going to be late. When the impatient Prince kept asking if we would begin, I devised a plan which (I hoped) would buy us some time and keep everyone in good humor. I asked the Prince and his guests to take their seats: the ceremonial feast was about to commence. In the kitchen tent, I mounted an enormous silver serving dish which was then covered with a muslin cloth. The ceremonial gong sounded; four bearers carried my five-foot-nine-inch, 145-pound body into the feasting tent; they set the wobbling tray in front of the Prince. The head cook announced that in honor of the occasion he had prepared a rare and special treat: "Athollian cous-cous." With a dramatic flourish he whisked the cloth into the air, revealing a slightly nervous majordomo trying to humor his employer. Crouched on my hands and knees in a white robe with an apple stuck between my teeth, I humbly performed my rendition of a stuffed lamb. Fortunately everyone laughed; the tension broke. Such a creative approach to problem-solving transformed a potentially volatile situation into an extremely enjoyable evening.

My grandfather, William Barber Cross, was a successful businessman who had inherited both money and property. He owned commercial businesses and real estate throughout England and enjoyed the fruits of his labor by living in grand style on a two-hundred-acre estate named Wentworth Park. His wife, Emma Louise Fielding Cross, had at one time been an actress who worked with a troupe of traveling performers called "Hailey's Juveniles." These troops were popular in the early 1900s, performing a variety of pantomimes and plays in small towns and villages. Hailey's Juveniles traveled extensively throughout England and Europe reciting Shakespeare; on one occasion they had even played before the Russian Czar. My grandmother, however, like most of her contemporaries, relinquished her career when she married. She became wife, mother, and hostess for over sixty years and spent her days organizing a household with a sizable staff.

Wentworth Park had been in our family since the sixteenth century. The estate was constructed on the ruins of a twelfth-century monastic retreat which had been destroyed during the reign of Henry VIII. The main house, a fifty-five-room Georgian structure built in elegant bathstone, proved to be a marvelous playground for children. Each room was like a passport to an exotic country. Several guest suites in the east wing of the house were named after my grandmother's favorite flowers. Sarah and I soon relabeled them and, with the assistance of a few props and a great deal of imagination, we transformed Emily Rose, Gardinia, Buttercup, and Lady Olivia into Paris, New York, Bombay, and Tokyo. Sarah pretended to be an internationally acclaimed actress or an elegant society matron on a world tour; I played the part of her faithful majordomo, fulfilling her every fancy.

Once a week my grandmother held bridge parties for the ladies in town. During these gatherings Sarah and I roamed throughout the house without worry of being detected. The attic was always one of the first stops on our itinerary; it contained trunks filled with theatrical costumes. My grandmother's three sisters, Nellie, Dollie, and Gussie, had also been actresses. When they gave up the grease paint, Wentworth Park became the storage facility for everything they had collected through the years: robes, ribbons, frilly gowns, shoes, masks, hats, wigs, makeup—anything they had purloined from the various plays they had each performed. One corner of the

6

room held an untold treasure of props which included a penny farthing (an antique bicycle with an enormous wheel in front and a small wheel in back), a collection of bottles, army uniforms, flags, fans, cribs, perambulators, and one of Sarah's favorite items: an antique wheelchair. Sarah loved to play Camille, feigning coughing fits and collapsing into the movable chair; in her last few dying breaths she would order me to push her across the creaky wooden floor "one last time."

With the short attention spans of children and so many rooms to stimulate our creativity, Wentworth Park certainly rivaled any amusement park. The conservatory full of white wicker furniture and a variety of plants became our Louisiana cotton plantation. We transformed the enormous drawing room with its oversized leather sofas and chairs into the lobby of Berlin's Grand Hotel. One of our favorite playgrounds, however, was the enormous and elegant ballroom which we converted into a make-believe skating pond. This space, which once entertained royalty and heads of state, comprised one entire wing of the main house but was rarely used anymore. Sarah and I would sneak inside and, in stocking feet, slide across the highly polished wooden floors. On several occasions we lost track of time; my grandmother would wander through Wentworth Park's cavernous halls trying to locate her two mini-explorers.

"Des-*mond?* Sa-*rah?*" she'd cry out, her voice raising an octave in pitch between the first and second syllables of our names. "Where have you two little monkeys disappeared to now? You're not rummaging again, are you? The devil finds mischief for idle hands!"

* * *

Twenty-foot-high iron gates and a pair of keepers' cottages protected the entranceway to Wentworth Park from any unwanted visitors. Those who had permission to approach the estate drove down a long, straight path surrounded by rolling meadows, lakes, and trees. The property contained riding stables, greenhouses, and facilities for a complete farm, which, in earlier days, supplied the household with much of its food.

Although the main house contained fifty-five rooms, we actually lived in eighteen. The days had long passed when my grandparents held a dinner for fifty in the formal dining-room or gave a grand party for four hundred in the ballroom. To be practical we used the family dining-room, which seated sixteen, and several of the small drawing rooms. Many sections of the house were sealed-off, the furniture dust-wrapped. My grandmother, ever the actress, loved to recount tales describing the grand parties she used to give, filling the house with a wide and wild assortment of artists and aristocrats. Since I had developed a taste for elegant parties at an early age, I felt frustrated by the fact that my late arrival had excluded me from such spectacular soirées. To appease myself, I persuaded Sarah to accompany me into the sealed-off sections, where we re-created the celebrations our grandmother had so dramatically described.

Even though a majority of the house was not used at the time I was in residence, the staff was still sizable. It consisted of: Charlotte, the cook and overall manageress; Anais, the maid; Mr. G (Gifford), the butler; Iris, the cleaning woman; Mrs. Musgrave, the housekeeper; Martha, the laundress; Nanny Maples, nanny and governess to both Sarah and myself; Jack (Charlotte's husband), the carpenter and handyman; Mr. B (Bellows), the gardener; and Alfred, the chauffeur and mechanic.

In addition to my grandparents, Sarah, and myself, my Uncle Roland lived in the house with his longtime companion, Philip. Roland and Philip were best friends as children; over the years their friendship evolved into a very loving relationship. They had an entire wing of Wentworth Park to themselves but took all of their meals with the family. Roland and Philip's relationship was accepted by everyone. In fact, homosexuality is quite accepted amongst the upper classes of British society. Money seems to have a way of stretching the tolerance level of even the most inflexible individuals.

Whenever my parents were in town they stayed in a separate wing of Wentworth Park. By my fourth year, however, they became infrequent visitors. My father was a diplomat who traveled frequently; my mother, Vera Louise, chose to accompany him. As a diplomat, my father was required to do a fair amount of entertaining; he needed his wife to act as hostess. But my mother, I believe, welcomed the opportunity to travel: She initially had a difficult time dealing with her children. Vera did not start her family until she was into her late thirties; I think motherhood proved to be more than she had bargained for. Up until that time, she had led an independent and spirited life. Vera was the kind of woman who had grown accustomed to being catered to and looked after. When she had her children and suddenly realized what was required of her, I think, like many first-time mothers, she felt frightened and unprepared.

*   *   *

9

My grandmother, or "Nansy" as I lovingly called her, became my mother figure and mentor. Standing on her toes, she reached just five-feet two-inches and sported a plump yet elegant figure. An angelic face truthfully represented a woman who never had a bad word to say about anyone. Influenced by a mother who was a concert pianist and a father who was a violinist, Nansy pursued those creative pleasures which the leisure of wealth brought her. She wrote plays and theatrical songs, embroidered pillowcases, and sculpted in clay. She was never happier than those days spent in her garden wearing an enormous white picture hat to shield her delicate skin from the sun. She also loved to paint; with an easel set-up under a large oak tree, she would work on landscapes or abstract creations.

Sometimes Nansy invited Sarah and me into the private sanctuary of her sitting room, where we were swallowed by large down-filled sofas covered in a yellow flowered print. We sank so far into the furniture our feet hung over the ends, never reaching the blue Persian carpet below. Nansy would tip-toe over to her Queen Anne cabinet and whisper our secret word ("babalamb"); as if by magic, the top opened and a tray popped up containing decanters, sherry glasses, and a bottle of Nansy's favorite beverage. As she hummed a lullaby and methodically poured herself a drink, I wondered if my grandfather was aware of his wife's secret treasure. Amidst a collection of carriage clocks and baskets filled with sewing, needlepoint, tatting, and crochet, Nansy held our hands and narrated enchanting tales about her days as an actress. One of her more thrilling sagas detailed the time she was smuggled out of Russia during the revolution. A beautiful princess on whose private estate the troop had been performing helped the young actors cross the border to safer territory.

The English have always been known for their eccentricities—especially amongst the upper classes. I have found that British aristocracy not only condones aberrant behavior but enthusiastically embraces the daily deviants: In the presence of such an unusual personality one is guaranteed a colorful evening or weekend in an otherwise dull and drafty manor house.

When my sister Sarah celebrated her fifth birthday no one thought it odd when I helped organize what today would be called a "drag" party: little boys came dressed as little girls and vice-versa. The idea originated one afternoon while my grandmother, Sarah, and myself were re-creating the adventures of Peter Pan. Very few characters in the history of dramatic literature fly through the air; I immediately recognized a rare opportunity. I was determined to soar through space unlike any other Peter Pan before me. Little did I know that my sister had set her sights on the same role. My grandmother/casting director very emphatically explained that the title character was always played by a girl, which in this case would be my sister.

"Beside which," she added, "Sarah's birthday is in two weeks. You should make every possible effort to indulge her."

I decided that if Sarah was awarded the best male part (I was unwilling to concede this dramaturgical point) then it was only fair that I should play all the best female roles: Wendy, Tinkerbell, and the mother. Our staging of

Peter Pan was to be the entertainment for Sarah's birthday party; we decided it would be great fun to have all our friends cross-dress and incorporate them into the show. On the day of the occasion, Sarah looked quite dashing in her green gymnastic suit with matching tights. I wore a long blonde wig, white lace and taffeta gown, and peep-toe shoes. Years later I was reminded of the costume when, while working for actress Marlo Thomas, she accused me of stealing one of her dresses. When I finally located the missing garment I told her, "It was ridiculous to accuse me because I never wear anything strapless!" The moment the words flew out of my mouth I remembered the taffeta gown. It had been twenty-seven years since I had last worn a dress.

My weekend sojourns to Wentworth Park were always the highlight of the week. But that is not surprising when one endures Monday through Friday tackling such stimulating subjects as Latin and logarithms. Sundays were my favorite: On this special day of the week everyone put on his or her Sunday best—jackets and ties for the gentlemen, frilly dresses for the ladies. We packed ourselves into either the Bentley S3 or the Jaguar and drove to a splendid country inn for luncheon. Sarah and I always sat in the back with Nansy; Uncle Roland and Philip joined Grandad up front. If the weather was chilly we buried ourselves under a fur car rug. No one ever spoke during the journey. We either read, watched passing scenery, or listened to classical music on the radio.

One of our favorite luncheon spots was "The Rising Sun at Hope" in a neighboring village. Although Sarah and I were very young, we were allowed one-half glass of wine (mixed with water) with our Sunday meal. I later learned that this is a common practice in Europe. But at the time Sarah and I believed that our weekly wine dosage pushed us onto the brink of adulthood. Our Sunday excursions helped us to feel very important and grownup. We were never looked down upon or treated as "children" but were always referred to as "young adults." Of course this was contingent upon the fact that we behaved properly. We were fortunate to have been loved and yet not spoiled by such extravagant surroundings. The rule of the house was respect for everyone and proper manners in everything we did. Grandad was the ruler of his kingdom whose word was law. In retrospect, I believe he was a fair and generous man who only wanted the very best for his family.

Two

My grandfather frequently traveled to London and other parts of the world for business purposes. It was not uncommon for him to arrive at the Chippendale breakfast table and, between spoonfuls of cornflakes, announce, "Emma, I'll be leaving for Europe today for three weeks. I won't be taking you with me this time."

Nansy, ever the agreeable soul, would sip her tea and politely reply, "All right, Barber." (She called him by his middle name.) "Look after yourself. Have a good journey."

There was never a confrontation between them or an unpleasant word spoken—not that I ever witnessed. My grandfather simply would not have allowed it. He felt that if something could not be communicated in a dignified tone then it was best left unstated. You can imagine my reaction years later when, while working for Saul Steinberg and Marlo Thomas—"the King and Queen of Scream"—shrieking obscenities were an everyday occurrence.

15

Much like students who feel uninhibited when the teacher leaves the classroom, Nansy, Sarah, and I would frolic in my grandfather's absence, in a manner he would never permit. The lack of an authority figure transformed Wentworth Park from a peaceful, dignified estate into the setting for a zany English farce. William Barber Cross was the sole adult in a house full of children and child-spirited adults. Although I loved my grandfather dearly, he was, nevertheless, a very strict and serious-minded gentleman who would have deemed our preferred behavior frivolous.

By the time I was nine, I had become quite proficient at playing "Mistress and Majordomo." With my grandfather away, I organized elegant dinners, complete with White Doulton china and original eighteenth-century Waterford glass. Nansy, Roland, Philip, Sarah, and I dressed in formal attire and dined at opposite ends of a magnificent fifty-foot table. Afterward we retired to the main drawing room where Nansy would sing the music of Gilbert and Sullivan in her lilting soprano. Roland played his clarinet, Philip accompanied on the Steinway grand, and Sarah and I, the designated drummers, tapped eighteenth-century silver against a white marble fireplace.

During my grandfather's absence Nansy would invite her two elder sisters to share a few days at Wentworth Park. Nellie and Gussie, both spinsters who had also enjoyed theatrical careers, were highly animated in both speech and behavior. They each owned identical over-sized raccoon coats and hats which made them resemble kindly old bears on the prowl. Nansy had made private arrangements for her sisters' financial security; they

16

never had to go without. A special bond existed between the three women: Individually incomplete, united they formed a circle of life and love which I was certain would rotate into infinity. As a child I felt that if I could stand in the midst of their circle I would be safe and happy forever. Perhaps it was the death of their fourth sister, Dolly, which bonded the other three. Dolly had also been an actress who, ironically, died on stage of a brain seizure at the age of thirty-six while singing a musical selection entitled "Goodbye Dolly."

With so many performers in the house it was inevitable that playacting would comprise a majority of our entertainment. And with an overflowing attic of costumes, makeup, and props it was only a matter of time before we formed our own in-house repertory company. We performed Nansy's original plays and popular musicals like *South Pacific*. We even revived our infamous "drag" version of *Peter Pan*. This time, however, Sarah got a bloody nose when she tried to fly; I finally persuaded my grandmother to let me perform the role and gracefully swayed from an apple tree in my green-dyed pajamas. These were truly times of magic for a child.

It wasn't long before I began to assist Charlotte in the kitchen; she willingly taught me her culinary secrets. With the assistance of my great-aunts I organized lavish costume parties from various historical periods. King Arthur's Court and Caligula's Rome were our two favorites; we repeated them on several occasions. The unbelievable sight of Nansy, Gussie, and Nellie dressed in form-fitting togas, performing an improvisational dance in the rose garden, is one I shall never forget. No matter what year in which we set our parties, however, the food remained in the twentieth century. Charlotte was not up to being a medieval cook nor was she excited at the prospect of wearing costumes—although she once agreed to trade in her traditional blue housecoat and white apron when we cast her as Marie Antoinette.

The presence of youngsters encouraged Nansy and her sisters to retain that sense of "play" which is at the heart of every actor—the ability to free oneself of adult-imposed inhibition and become a child once again. It is this very quality which adults so quickly relinquish and then later desperately try to rediscover. A pop psychologist has had enormous success addressing this issue, teaching adults how to overcome depression and dissatisfaction by recognizing that "we are all still divine infants in exile." I was fortunate to have learned the lesson many years ago amidst a collection of eccentric and fun-loving English ladies.

All of our madcap merriment came to an abrupt halt as soon as we heard Grandad was due home. He would not have been pleased if he had learned even half of what transpired in his absence. The aunts were quickly packed into the Bentley; costumes, props, and makeup were hidden away in the attic; the house was restored to a place of quiet meditation and would so remain until my grandfather's next business trip.

Ours was a remarkably different home when my grandfather traveled. Nansy was more lively and free spirited— like a young school girl on the brink of discovering the secret mystery of boys. There was an extra skip in her step and a devilish twinkle in her eye as she dreamed up each new adventure. Once when I was eight I asked her why it couldn't always be this way. She became very still and looked slightly sad. Gently taking my face into two very loving hands, she peered into my eyes and whispered, "If you dare to be who you truly want to be, you risk enjoying every day of your life." She spoke with such quiet intensity I was initially frightened. Of course, I didn't understand what she meant at the time. But as I grew older, I gradually began to realize what she was trying to communicate. During my grandfather's business trips I watched my grandmother's transformation from a tamed white dove into a colorful strutting peacock. But as soon as the master of the house returned his most prized bird flew back into her cage and quietly closed the door.

Nansy had every possible comfort imaginable. She never worried about finances, often traveling to London for the day without a pound in her purse. Everything was taken care of so that she didn't have to concern herself with such mundane thoughts as money. But it became apparent to me that she had paid a price: unlike her philosophy, she had *not* dared to be her *true* self but had veered off the path into another direction. Her situation was not unique for a woman of her time, or even for men and women of today. We all make choices which entail sacrifices and compromises. And it is difficult to ascertain at any given moment whether we have paid too high a price. Only after years of life experience can we look back and evaluate our choices. The older I grew, however, and the more I observed my grandmother, I began to wonder if she had sacrificed too much for domestic security. Her words of advice would haunt me and make a distinct impression on how I would approach my life and career.

* * *

Our days at Wentworth Park always followed the same schedule: breakfast at 8:15 A.M.; lunch at 1:15 P.M.; afternoon tea at 4:00 P.M.; and at precisely 6:30 P.M., everyone was dressed for dinner and the cocktail hour began.

Dinner was a formal occasion: Gentlemen wore black-tie if there were guests, otherwise a tie and jacket. Nansy outfitted herself in exquisite gowns, which were created in London. If she was feeling particularly adventurous and couldn't suppress her creative urges she would rummage through her theatrical wardrobe and dress in an old costume. My grandfather always humored her on these occasions, acting as if it was perfectly normal to have one's wife dressed as Cleopatra for dinner. One evening my grandmother's choice of clothing catapulted Sarah and me into an uncontrollable giggle fit. Nansy majestically descended the wooden staircase dressed as Mary Queen of Scots. Her ensemble consisted of an enormous gown with a ruffled neck and petticoats, and a bejeweled tiara resting on a lacquered wig, accessorized by a single strand of pearls. My grandfather, without so much as raising an eyebrow or flaring a nostril, said, "You look very nice, dear. Ready for your usual sherry?" I later wondered if my grandmother dressed in such a fashion in an attempt to provoke a reaction out of her poker-faced husband. If that was her motive, she was never successful.

Ten minutes before the cocktail hour began Mr. G would roll the grog tray into the library. It contained two blocks of ice, glasses, an assortment of liquor bottles and accompanying garnishes. Grandad drank scotch and never exceeded his one-drink limit. Roland and Philip preferred gin and could not even spell the word "limit"—

although they never behaved in a drunken fashion. And Nansy would quietly sip as many glasses of sherry as she could politely consume. Nansy loved her sherry; in addition to the private stash in her sitting room, she kept a few bottles hidden around the house so that she could partake of her favorite beverage whenever the mood struck. Sarah and I usually sipped fizzy water in a martini glass. We had seen this once in a London play and thought it was terribly sophisticated. By the respective ages of eight and ten, Sarah and I were desperate in our attempts to be cultured; our grandparents kindly humored us.

Dinner was served promptly at 7:30 P.M. One instinctively knew what day of the week it was by the menu (which only changed if we were entertaining). It usually went as follows:

Sunday:	Roast beef, roast pork, or roast lamb rotated on a weekly basis. If we went out for lunch (which we frequently did during the summer) the roast was missed one week.
Monday:	Shepherd's pie
Tuesday:	Pork chops unless we'd had roast pork on Sunday in which case it would be lamb chops
Wednesday:	Steak and kidney pie
Thursday:	Roast chicken
Friday:	Fish
Saturday:	Cold chicken (Charlotte's day off)

21

A typical menu for a four-course formal dinner would consist of smoked salmon, cream of watercress soup, roast pheasant, and trifle, followed by cheese and fruit. It is customary at a formal dinner party for the ladies to retire into the drawing room, leaving the gentlemen to drink brandy, smoke cigars, tell off-color stories, and amuse themselves with other such manly fun. At the appropriate time the hostess would rise and say, "Ladies, shall we retire to the withdrawing room?" The gentlemen would stand until their feminine counterparts had left the room. It is considered very bad manners to leave the table during dinner for *any* reason.

In the drawing room the ladies would have coffee and liqueurs (usually sherry) and converse amongst themselves. As a child I found the men's conversation boring, so I frequently wandered back and forth between the two groups. After approximately thirty minutes, the gentlemen would join the ladies in the withdrawing room; everyone generally departed before midnight.

During dinner it was considered vulgar to mention money, religion, sex, or politics. Suitable conversation topics were travel, art, theatre, the weather, horticulture, and horses. It was the hostess' job to keep the conversation flowing and to try to include each of her guests. She was allowed to change any topic which she deems unsuitable for polite dinner conversation.

A highly skilled hostess is like an air traffic controller: She monitors all the pieces of information in the air at any given moment and makes split-second decisions about which news item may land safely at her table.

*   *   *

I was fascinated with beautiful automobiles at an early age. Being raised in an environment with a grandfather who collected fine cars certainly fueled that interest. When I became a proficient driver (at the age of thirteen) I began to play chauffeur to Nansy while Grandad was away. She would sit in the back and announce various destinations on the estate via the intercom, always stressing that I should proceed with extreme caution. My grandfather loved his cars as much as he loved his family; the slightest scratch would be just cause for banishment from Wentworth Park.

At fourteen, I began assisting in the supervision of Wentworth Park while my grandparents were away. They soon realized that I was a born organizer with a pleasant and out-going personality. It was not as strange as it may seem to entrust certain aspects of running a large estate to an adolescent—especially in England and Europe where children mature at a quicker rate than in America.

Whenever my grandparents traveled they were accompanied by a maid, valet, and a dozen large wardrobe steamer trunks. They relaxed in suites on popular luxury liners, cruising through exotic waters. In the spring they vacationed at their Italian villa in Diana Marina, midway between Monte Carlo and Genoa. The one summer I visited them they had recently acquired an adorable two-month-old tiger cub which Nansy named Felicity. Unfortunately, when the over-affectionate cat grew to full size, they had to place her in a zoo: It was exceedingly difficult to keep a household staff with a full, grown tiger roaming through the villa.

*   *   *

Christmas was the highlight of each year at Wentworth Park. Mr. B and his boys would hoist a thirty-foot tree into the great hall. Nansy, Roland, Philip, Sarah, and I decorated the massive evergreen with antique ornaments and candles, which were not lit until our Christmas Eve celebration. The entire staff and their families were invited. My mother played the piano while Nansy sang "Silent Night." Then everyone would join in for a selection of festive carols. Nansy and Grandad gave every man, woman, and child a gift. My grandmother remembered everyone by name, a remarkable achievement considering the size of the crowd and her advanced years. The household staff each received a Christmas bonus. After the gift-giving, a buffet supper of champagne, sherry, beer, and mince pies was served. At the end of our celebration the candles were ceremoniously extinguished. When I was twelve, however, we started using electric lights: The tree had caught fire the previous year during Nansy's rendition of "Silent Night." A true performer, she hated to be upstaged by anyone or anything—even a fire. Nansy banished candles from future celebrations, declaring that they were no longer safe.

I was fortunate in that during my teen-age years no one pressured me into making choices about my future. Nansy continued to echo her philosophy about being true to oneself; she encouraged me to explore all options before locking myself into any specific career. Most of my classmates at boarding school were under constant pressure to commit to a particular path and make the appropriate choice for university. At first I thought I would become a veterinarian because I loved animals. Later I thought I might enjoy being an archaeologist. It still had never occurred to me that I might become a majordomo and receive payment for what I did freely for my family.

As my grandparents approached their eighties, I noticed that they were gradually slowing down and becoming less active. Watching someone you love grow old can be a frustratingly painful experience. There is nothing anyone can do to stop the aging process; yet somehow we all feel compelled to try. I pity the child who has lost a parent early on in life; yet I envy his never having to witness a life slowly lose its many shadings until it is reduced to a few primary colors. I watched a highly spirited woman who had once danced wildly in a garden dressed in a toga become unwilling to leave her house for fear she might fall and break a bone. I wasn't certain if I should indulge her fears or yank her out of an ever-growing complacency and thrust her back into life. My grandparents reached that difficult stage where many of their contemporaries had passed away; suddenly they were confronted with their own mortality.

Just when I felt I had grasped the situation and accepted the inevitable process of aging, something unexpected happened which irrevocably altered all our lives. My uncle Roland was diagnosed with cancer at the age of forty-nine. Three months later he died in his mother's arms in his Wentworth Park bedroom. (Philip stayed on at the house until he suffered a heart attack and passed away two years after Roland's death.) Roland was the golden-haired boy with the ebullient smile who personified my grandparents' hope for the continued success of the family business. My mother had no interest in taking over; I was much too young to be put in charge—and I preferred organizing households to businesses. Sadly, with no one willing or able to carry on the work, all the family businesses were sold.

Shortly thereafter, my grandparents held a family meeting and announced that they were thinking of selling Wentworth Park. The estate had become too large and unmanageable for them; it held sad memories and they felt it was time to move on. Many of the staff members who had devoted a lifetime of service to my family were ready to retire. Grandad asked if anyone would like to be gifted the estate, knowing none of us was in a financial position to maintain the property. We all declined. And on that day in 1969, after the estate's having been in our family for over four hundred years, the monumental decision to sell Wentworth Park was made.

It was the end of an era not only for my family but also for a certain way of life in England. Very few families could afford to live on such large estates anymore, passing them down from one generation to the next. These large estates were frequently divided and sold off in pieces. The old style of living—which had defined the majority of my grandparents' years—was replaced by a new, more efficient way of life. My grandfather's small businesses were being devoured by huge conglomerates. And like an elegantly crafted sand castle, which time and the elements slowly erode, the style and manner in which my grandparents had lived was quietly disappearing.

Nansy and Grandad relocated to a fifteen-room estate, but their hearts were not in the move. Roland's unexpected death had irreparably damaged their spirits. I had just graduated and was rapidly approaching my eighteenth birthday. Something powerful stirred within me, fueled by my grandmother's haunting words of advice. I felt compelled to do something daring with my life. I wasn't quite sure what it would be at the time, but I thought London might provide the answer. Grandad initially was not pleased with my lack of direction, but after Roland's death he was far more flexible about everything. Nansy was delighted with my plans (or lack thereof). She believed that after so many years of sitting in classrooms, the best education was life experience through a series of travels and adventures. My parents said they would support me in whatever I decided to do. So off to London I went.

Grandad gave me the choice of his Belgravia townhouse or a flat in nearby Chelsea. I opted for the flat: a townhouse was far too formal for a seventeen-year-old young man with no specific plans. I received a monthly allowance from the family trust for a one-year period. Both my parents and grandparents encouraged me to take my time and try and discover exactly what I wanted to do. Little did I know that I was already performing my chosen profession. I just wasn't being paid for it. But that would come soon enough.

Three

In the spring of 1970, I moved to London to pursue those career-potential areas which were stimulating, creative, and fun. Cooking certainly fulfilled the three requirements. Under Charlotte's expert tutelage I had learned to prepare plain family fare for groups of from five to fifty. Having mastered the art of mashed tatties with brown gravy, I felt primed to conquer new culinary horizons. Cordon Bleu was "all the rage" in Europe; I decided to train with a proper Cordon Bleu chef.

The French term was originally coined by Louis XV. The story goes that he had a large and jovial cook whose efforts so pleased him one day, he announced, "Je vous donnez le cordon bleu" (I give you the blue ribbon). Henceforth, the chef's cooking style became known as Cordon Bleu. This particular cuisine is characterized by soufflés, sauces, and a generous use of cream, eggs, butter, and wine. Because we currently live in a health-conscious age, people rarely eat Cordon Bleu on a daily basis anymore. The cholesterol and calorie count for an average three-course meal would give the most lenient nutritionist a permanent case of the shudders. But in 1970 Cordon Bleu was considered "de rigueur" by the upper classes of British and European society; it remained quite popular in America until a few years ago.

I studied for six months with an extremely high-strung but competent chef who taught me the secret mysteries of French cuisine. Monsieur Chevin was an award-winning cook who for some unknown reason, always spoke in questions, utilizing the pronoun "we."

"Are we having success deglazing the pan today? Did we remember to beat the eggs in one at a time? Must we chatter incessantly while we perform our work?"

I concluded that Monsieur Chevin must have dropped out of his English class shortly after the lesson in interrogative sentences. Despite a few quirky characteristics he was a very thorough instructor. During my training I learned to prepare a variety of pastries, breads, soups, sauces, terrines, pâtés, soufflés, mousses, wonderful chicken dishes, ragouts of beef and lamb, and hors d'oeuvres to delight the most exacting gourmet.

Armed with an array of new cooking skills and money to invest from the family trust, I opened a small restaurant called "Ashley's Pantry" with a take-away shop next door. This was considered quite daring in 1970: Take-away was almost unheard of in England at the time. The restaurant was located in Bath, a sophisticated and historical city characterized by an affluent, trendy society. Ashley's Pantry featured a combination of gourmet and Mediterranean-style food served in a simple yet elegant environment.

I planned a large party for the opening and sent hundreds of invitations to everyone I could think of. Unfortunately, I neglected to examine the printer's proofs before mailing them out. Imagine my surprise when one of Nansy's friends telephoned to say she would be delighted to attend the opening but wondered why I had named my establishment "Ashley's *Panties.*"

Both the restaurant and take-away business were prosperous from the start. I credited a majority of the success to a hard-working, caring, and experienced staff well treated in all respects. My experiences at Wentworth Park had prepared me for working with others. I learned that if you speak kindly to your employees, treat them with respect, and let them know their efforts are appreciated, they will enthusiastically commit to the task at hand. Most people, unfortunately, work for either indifferent or abusive employers who regard their subordinates as interchangeable commodities. A truly successful employer is one who has the ability to make each employee feel special—as if he or she uniquely contributes something meaningful to the whole. I was fortunate to have had grandparents who set such a fine example.

After my first successful year in business I decided to branch out into home catering. My initial assignments came via word of mouth through many noble families in the area—some of whom I had grown up with and knew quite intimately. Years later, when I moved to Los Angeles and recounted my history, someone asked if I didn't find it embarrassing cooking and serving people I knew personally. It was the first time I encountered the difference between the American and European perceptions of domestic employment. In England or in Europe it is not considered beneath oneself to enter into a domestic position. The offspring of many titled families have, at eighteen, become nannies to other families or worked as a cook/housekeeper in villas or ski châteaux. Some seek employment as crew members on yachts, grooms in stables, or companions to the elderly. Sarah Ferguson was a housekeeper in a fashionable Swiss ski resort before becoming the Duchess of York. Young people are encouraged to work—to contribute in some form; they are brought up to be independent and self-sufficient as soon as possible. These jobs can actually be quite fun while contemplating what to do with one's future.

On several occasions while I was living in Manhattan I felt that certain individuals looked down upon my chosen profession. After learning of my upbringing they couldn't fathom why I wanted to work as a "servant." They didn't appreciate the fine art involved in creating a perfect meal or setting a beautiful table. I found it ironic that the very people who judged me wanted the benefit of my training and experience when it came to their own households. Most of them didn't have a clue as to how to manage a staff of ten or organize a dinner party for fifty. Yet they felt superior because they earned their money in such prestigious fields as sales or spouse-hunting.

Lady Edith Foxwell, the Earl of Lambert's daughter, requested my catering services on numerous occasions. I met the sixty-year-old grande dame at a dinner party and found her eccentric and charming. Edith was a striking woman with a wild mane of red hair which she dramatically tossed to emphasize a point. She had previously been married to Ivor Foxwell, the director of such highly respected films as *The Cruel Sea*. Since her divorce, how-

32

ever, Edith had committed her life to exploring the secret mysteries of youth through a series of relationships with young men. Her most recent acquisition was an Adonis-like Brazilian named Carlos. Although only twenty-two, Carlos had learned a few of life's more pleasurable "secrets," which he was only too willing to share with Edith.

Unlike other women her age, Edith was neither embarrassed by nor did she feel the need to hide her young escorts. Quite the contrary: She loved defying convention and openly paraded her boys about town. Although this set a few Victorian tongues a-tittering, Edith was, nevertheless, invited with her escort of the moment to every social event of any kind. She was, after all, the daughter of an Earl and immensely wealthy: two very strong calling cards under any circumstances.

When questioned about her taste for the "colts" (which is how her horse-breeding friends referred to the young men), Edith would laugh and say her contemporaries either had their lovers on the sly or couldn't get them for love *or* money. I think most of her female critics were both fascinated and frightened by the prospect of such a young lover. They certainly never lost an opportunity to interrogate me about the intimate details of Edith's sex life—not that I ever revealed anything. I'm certain, however, if any of her critics pulled back the covers one hot summer's night and discovered the warm, pulsating body of a strapping youth, she would have screamed until her hair net fell off, running madly in the opposite direction.

Edith adored entertaining at Sherston Farm, her large country estate in Wiltshire. She was extremely gregarious and reminded me at times of my great aunts, Nellie and

Gussie. Her estate contained an enormous swimming pool (quite unusual in England) with a poolside telephone hidden in the deck and a built-in stereo system throughout the grounds—very Hollywood for an Englishwoman. Her guests ranged from pop stars to visiting heads of state. We used to joke that Edith's home was like England's version of the United Nations. One particular weekend she invited an Eastern dictator and his wife to a birthday celebration. Early that morning I walked into the breakfast room to inspect the table setting and discovered the couple in a prone position, praying to a blank television screen. Many of her friends were from the entertainment industry, although she was very close to the Duchess of Argyle and the most prominent members of England's aristocratic society. Each year she attended the Royal Garden Party and sat in the Royal Enclosure at Ascot.

The menus for Edith's dinner parties were often simple. She favored osso buco (veal knuckles), blanquette de veau, welsh rarebit (as a savory rather than a pudding), and chicken transformed in any one of a hundred different ways. For pudding she preferred my homemade banana and walnut ice cream with hot chocolate sauce, strawberry mousse, or lemon soufflé.

One of Edith's most admirable qualities was her ability to act quickly in a crisis. While I was working on the estate a friend of hers became entangled in an embarrassing situation; she helped him hide until it all blew over. At the time, a national scandal in Bath was one of the most talked-about events in the United Kingdom. Bath had become a very trendy spot for "the rich young things," attracting people like actress Helen Mirren, who had invested in a restaurant near mine. Several of these young socialites lived in communal style, sharing a country house called "Surrendell Farm." No one took much notice until Princess Margaret paid a weekend visit to see her friend Roddy Llewellyn. Wherever princesses go, the press soon follows. Reporters had a field day romantically linking Roddy and the Princess. The story was quite ridiculous. The press descended, nevertheless, and Roddy needed somewhere to hide.

Edith, who was well acquainted with his father, offered Roddy immediate sanctuary. No one would have suspected her: She lived an open life and collected such a bizarre assortment of people at her country home it seemed the last place anyone would attempt to hide. I owned a secluded mill house on the river, several miles off the main road. Edith proposed that if the press discovered Roddy at Sherston Farm I should hide him in *my* house. I told her it was highly unlikely he would be uncovered, but if necessary, I would rise to the occasion like a true espionage agent.

One day Edith asked me to escort her to the estate of Elliott and Patty Roosevelt—son and daughter-in-law to the ex-president. They had recently fled Portugal (which was going through a political upheaval) and had rented a large home in Wiltshire. I thought it rather odd as we approached the house to see a large American flag flapping in the wind. Edith made the proper introductions; Patty fervently shook my hand and offered me a drink in a distinctively American accent. I asked for a gin and tonic and received, what I assumed was the Lone Star version: The glass was so large and jam-packed with ice cubes it stuck to my hand. As I stated earlier, *everything* in polite English society is specifically defined—even the correct number of ice cubes which should be placed in a drink. Two ice cubes would be a perfectly acceptable number, three if one is feeling wildly extravagant. Anything more would be considered vulgar. Patty, of course, was just being hospitable, but her over-generous use of ice would certainly be frowned upon by the aristocracy.

My eyes quickly roamed the drawing room and froze upon a rather unusual piece of furniture. Directly in front of the fireplace sat a large black saddle mounted on an ivory base. Was this some strange type of Texas coffee table? A loving memorial to a dearly departed horse? A southern version of a love seat? Patty soon resolved the equestrian mystery: She suggested we make ourselves comfortable and then proceeded to straddle the monstrosity. I thought under the circumstances it would have been appropriate to ride English (side-saddle) but Patty apparently felt that her form-fitting riding breeches gave her the freedom to make herself at home. As she sipped a glass of scotch and told us stories about her travels, I felt certain that the talkative Texan was as close to American royalty as I would ever get.

England's shooting season is a major social event. It commences with the August grouse shoots in Scotland and continues through late winter. Shoots are highly organized social and sporting events where generation upon generation of aristocratic families intermingle on large country estates. Although the weather is always cold and wet for the start of the grouse season, the highest socially ranked individuals make every effort to attend. The shooting season gradually travels south and, depending upon the month, may include duck, pheasant, partridge, woodcock, and stag. During the various seasons it is customary to give large parties on one's estate for the purpose of celebrating the sport. The film *The Shooting Party*, set in Edwardian England, depicts this aspect of British society quite accurately.

I catered one of my first shoots at Castle Ashby, home of the Marquis and Marchioness of Northampton. The Marquis was first married to the Marquis of Bath's sister. He divorced her and then married a country girl who bore him four children when he was in his sixties. After several years, he divorced the mother of his children and married Effy, the third and last Marchioness of Northampton. They were both severe individuals who always dressed formally: country clothes during the day, evening wear at night. They had very little contact with their household staff; most requests were channeled through Garbert, the head butler who had been with the Marquis for decades. Each morning, the Marchioness spent fifteen minutes in the kitchen discussing menus.

The Northamptons entertained forty to fifty guests for a shooting party weekend in a grand and lavish style with beautifully prepared food. Although the menu for these events is standard I, nevertheless, reviewed each particular item with the Marchioness.

On the Wednesday before the scheduled shooting party was to commence, my assistant and I arrived at the castle to begin preparing the food. The Northamptons were knee-deep in help; my job was to oversee the staff and make certain all of the plans pertaining to food and table presentation were properly executed. These events involved a great deal of organization and could easily cost thousands of pounds, but money was never discussed.

Shoots are made up of three types of individuals: shooters—those invited guests (mostly men) actually participating in the shoot; loaders—those who carry the guns and ammunition and make sure the shooter always has a loaded gun; and beaters—usually a collection of local village lads who flush the birds out of the fields with sticks.

The morning of the shoot is always a time of frenzied activity. The gentlemen start the day with a hearty breakfast consisting of eggs, sausage, bacon, ham, stewed tomatoes, porridge, cold cereal, toast, coffee, and tea. As soon as they're packed into jeeps and driven to the fields, workmen begin to construct tents for the luncheon. The women usually sit in the drawing room or garden and read or politely converse until luncheon is served. I would supervise teams of up to fifteen kitchen workers, methodically reviewing my checklists throughout the day. Butlers and footmen set-up tables covered in crisp white linen and carefully arranged cut glass champagne glasses, fine china, and silver. The menu consisted of pasties (pastry dough filled with meat and potatoes), duck and hare terrines, game pies, steak and kidney pies, and ragout of lamb. All of the food was transported steaming hot from the main kitchen to the tents by Land-Rovers. After lunch, the men would return to the fields for a few more hours until it was time for tea.

Dinners were held in the banquet hall, which contained enormous family portraits and artwork from centuries of collecting. The fifty-foot dining table was set with priceless china (original Limoges or Crown Derby), gold tablewear, and eighteenth-century glass. The dinner menu consisted of smoked salmon, venison casserole, roast pheasant, welsh rarebit, lemon mousse, and steaming hot Grand Marnier soufflé.

These shooting weekends were not as lavish with the younger generation, however. When I worked with the Northamptons they were in their eighties and, as I had witnessed with my grandparents, their style of living and entertaining was gradually becoming extinct. I believe that after they both passed away, the heir, the Earl Spencer Compton, chose to live in a large house on the estate; the castle was opened to the public.

During my period of free-lance catering I arranged several parties for Lord and Lady Tollermache. They owned an enchanting residence in Suffolk where swans majestically glided across a lily-padded moat. Adjoining their estate was a large deer park where, in the appropriate season, hunts were held to cull the deer. This is a process of shooting specific deer to safeguard against overpopulation.

The first party I catered for the Tollermaches was during one such hunt. One afternoon, while organizing the final dinner preparations, I realized I would have to make a minor menu substitution; I felt it would be appropriate to inform Lady Tollermache. After diligently searching throughout the house, I couldn't find her anywhere. I located the head butler, explained my predicament, and asked him if he had any clues as to where I might find the mistress of the house. He smiled and quickly jotted down a list of directions. I followed the map which led to an unassuming door at the end of a long corridor on the second floor. Although I was certain I had made a wrong turn somewhere, I decided to investigate further, tapping gently on the wooden door frame.

"Yes, enter please," a small voice cried out.

I opened the door to a room which was completely dark except for a small light in the corner. Lady Tollermache sat wrapped from head-to-toe in a quilt, a book resting on her lap. She explained that although she knew the hunts were necessary, she was unnerved by the sights and sounds of killing deer. Every year, she shut herself away until the unpleasant ordeal was over.

Sir Cecil Beaton and I enjoyed a brief tenure together. He was a highly acclaimed photographer to the royal family as well as the set designer for the successful musical *My Fair Lady*. Sir Cecil was a well-mannered gentleman with exquisite taste and a beautiful home. His favorite hobby, aside from photography, was gardening. The first time I drove along the entranceway to Sir Cecil's country estate I spotted an elderly gentleman in a large picture hat carrying a flower basket in one hand and clipping shears in the other. The unassuming gardener was none other than Sir Cecil Beaton gathering peonies for a flower arrangement.

I catered a few parties for the elegant gentleman at Reddish House in Wiltshire. Although I found Sir Cecil charming, working at Reddish House proved to be a trying experience. His secretary, Edna, was an aging prima donna who had devoted her life to serving Sir Cecil. I'm certain Edna felt she was merely performing her duty and protecting her employer, but I found her meddlesome and overbearing. Edna made it quite clear that every detail pertaining to Sir Cecil's life required her approval. If for any reason one tried to circumvent her authority, Edna would in turn circumvent all sense of British decorum.

Despite Edna's insistence, I preferred to deal directly with Sir Cecil; he welcomed my company. We had great fun planning the menu and arrangements for a particular social occasion. As soon as Edna found out, however, she was livid. After repeatedly chastising me she changed all of the arrangements, stating that only *she* knew what was best for Sir Cecil.

Most of the parties I catered for the flamboyant photographer were attended by men. He was well known for his proclivity toward young and beautiful examples of the male gender. Despite his sexual preferences, he was friendly with everyone who was anyone in society. I wish our tenure could have been longer, but dealing with Edna was more than I could endure. Sir Cecil was an extremely polite, witty, and entertaining employer who quickly became addicted to my chocolate soufflé.

Four

By the end of 1971 my restaurant and take-away business were still running at a profit. I promoted two of my employees to co-manage the establishments while I continued to focus my energies on catering. Each party was an adventure into the great English unknown. Imagine being paid to help create a fantasy for someone with unlimited funds. Admittedly, the work was hard and harried at times, but it was never boring. And because I knew many of my employers socially, I was often a guest as well as a worker at these functions. Others may have been put off by this particular arrangement, but I loved it. Each occasion presented me with an opportunity to create a delectable menu, an exquisite table setting, and a festive environment. Bringing my vision of perfection into an employer's home was immensely satisfying.

My transition into becoming a majordomo grew out of the catering work. I organized several parties for a quaint lady named Dottie Sloan and her boorish husband Richard—a Mummy's Boy if ever there was one. Shortly after they were married, Richard's mother gave Dottie formal instruction on how to properly prepare her son's breakfast: "Eggs should be boiled for precisely 150 seconds; toast points must be lightly buttered with the crusts removed." Richard's mother was a very exacting woman.

The Sloans lived in a renovated Tudor manor called Covington Court. The grounds were extensive and included stables, meadows, a monks (fish) pond, yew hedges shaped into a maze, and beautifully sculpted gardens.

Dottie was impressed by my organizational abilities. Convinced that my skills could be applied to more than party-giving, Dottie offered me the use of a lovely house on the estate if, in addition to catering weekend parties, I would oversee certain aspects of running her household. I briefly mulled over the benefits of the proposal: with Monday through Thursday to myself I would be able to keep an eye on the restaurant, pursue additional catering possibilities, and cultivate other interests. The deciding factor, however, was my affection for Dottie, a lovely woman who had a great propensity for enjoying life. In the spring of 1972 I accepted the offer and became a nineteen-year-old "part-time" majordomo.

Dottie and Richard were members of the "horsey" set: a group of affluent individuals who bred, raised, and raced horses. The Sloans were quite successful in their efforts. One year their prized yearling placed at Royal Ascot, the most prestigious racing event of the year. Royal Ascot, founded in 1711 by Queen Anne, is also the most important social event of the racing season. In June of each year, the British class system is clearly defined by who receives invitations to enter The Royal Enclosure: a roped-off area where rich, royal, and aristocratic types celebrate in style. The Queen, Prince Philip, the Queen Mum and all the royals are usually in attendance, which is what makes Ascot such a socially significant event. Status-hungry individuals frequently try to "gate crash," but security is always at a maximum. I received an invitation to The Royal Enclosure a few times during the seventies, and was surprised to discover that the horse race was quite incidental to the party—an endless flow of champagne, caviar, strawberries, and people-watching.

Gentlemen at Ascot traditionally dress in morning suits (tail coats), striped pants, ascots, and grey top hats. The ensemble is frequently accessorized by a silver-topped cane. Ladies don extravagant and whimsical hats which have been specially created for the occasion—similar to the hats on display during New York City's Easter Parade. A typical headpiece might be shaped like a television set, sculpted into a national monument, or covered with enough fruit to feed a third-world nation. At Royal Ascot there is no such thing as a too outrageous chapeau.

Other noteworthy racing events for the season include: The Gold Cup at Cheltnam, a spa town at the edge of the Cotswolds; Aintree in Liverpool, which stages the Grand National—the premier national hunt season event every April; and Epson, near London.

The Sloans resided in their London townhouse Monday through Thursday and spent weekends at Covington Court. In addition to catering parties, I was responsible for supervising the household staff. Dottie was an interior designer and had been commissioned by her husband's company to transform the British painter Millet's old

45

house at Palace Gate into a magnificent office complex. She was well-bred and elegant; her name frequently appeared on the Sunday *Times* best-dressed list. Dottie's residences were beautifully decorated and immaculately maintained, which certainly simplified my job. The secret to running any size home—from a two-bedroom cottage in the Caribbean to a thirty-four room fortress on Fifth Avenue—is to organize it from top to bottom and then adhere to a strict set of maintenance standards. I have learned through experience, however, that cleanliness is in the eye of the beholder; there are certain small yet significant "household violations" which are invisible to the untrained eye. Such violations might include: discolored, scratched, or blemished walls; doors, glass surfaces, or mirrors with fingerprints; dust-covered tables or countertops; bathroom fixtures which are dull or covered with water spots; food substances of any kind on the cooker; disorganized cupboards and pantries; odors emanating from the refrigerator; closets which haven't been color-coordinated and separated by seasons; lint on the rugs and furniture—the list is virtually endless. Marlo Thomas, a true perfectionist if ever there was one, is the only employer I have ever worked for who had an "eye" which equalled mine. She could spot a wrinkled bedsheet or a slightly askew place setting from fifty paces.

I catered extremely lavish parties for the Sloans. Richard filled the manor with his nouveau riche friends—many of whom Dottie disapproved but, being a well-bred hostess, tolerated. She once confided in me that she wished they spoke more softly and didn't talk quite so much about their money.

Many of the Sloans' parties occurred during the fox

hunting season. The official opening is December 26, Boxing Day. During a typical hunt, the master blows his horn, signifying the start. Everyone cries, "Tally ho!"; with the hounds (traditionally beagles) leading the way, the group gallops off in search of the fox. The sport is in the chase rather than the kill. When the hounds have cornered their prey they (rather gruesomely) tear it to pieces. The animal's tail is traditionally awarded to the newest member of the hunt, who is then ceremoniously annointed on the forehead with the fox's blood.

Each winter the Duke and Duchess of Beaufort sponsor The Beaufort Hunt. Only those individuals who stable their horses within twenty miles of the hunt headquarters can participate in this event. The Hunt Ball is the social highlight of the season and is held in a different location each year. The rich give spectacular dinner parties before the Ball, making it a very profitable time of year for caterers.

During my first year with the Sloans, Dottie volunteered the use of her ballroom at Covington Court for The Hunt Ball. I spent weeks laboriously preparing the house and ordering all of the necessary provisions. At 10:00 P.M. on the evening of the Ball, the guests began to arrive. They danced to the music of a live band, drank glasses bubbling with Taittinger, and reviewed the events of the hunt. It stormed wildly that particular evening; although the roof leaked and the heat broke down, no one even flapped. The guests accepted such inconveniences as part of country living and consumed more champagne to placate themselves. At 4 A.M. I (and several helpers) laid out a buffet breakfast consisting of smoked salmon, scrambled eggs, caviar, sausages, bacon, toast, coffee, tea, orange juice, and champagne. By 6:00 A.M. everyone went home and I went to bed.

Dottie and I both shared a love of animals. I adored her pets: a golden retriever named Rubert Bear; a black labrador named Mandy; and an adorable white rat named Horace who, much to the horror of Dottie's guests, had free run of the house. Horace was a handsome creature with pink eyes, long white whiskers, and a charming temperament. He was Dottie's constant companion. Whenever she traveled the 110 miles between London and Covington Court, Horace would sit perched on Dottie's shoulder or snuggled into the pocket of her mink— depending upon the season.

I first met Horace while seated upon a green leather sofa in the Sloan's drawing room. During my conversation I felt something tickling my neck. Imagine my surprise when I looked down and saw a rat nibbling my earlobe. I didn't mind: I had kept mice and hamsters as a child.

Not everyone, however, took Horace's overaffectionate nature to heart. One afternoon I was serving a very formal tea to a room full of society matrons. Horace (who had an affinity for mink) decided to take a nap on Lady Hermione's sable-collared jacket. As soon as this dignified matron saw what she termed "a vile and filthy rodent attaching itself to my personage," she began to run around the drawing room performing her imitation of a high-speed hula dancer.

Dottie, ever the polite hostess, nonchalantly said, "Silly, silly, Horace. Now do be a good boy and stop bothering poor Lady Hermione." Dottie attempted to calm her flabbergasted guest, who was embarrassed by her loss of composure. "You'll find he really is very sweet once you become better acquainted. Come to Mummy," she cooed, waiving her beautifully manicured fingernails. Horace scampered onto Dottie's lap and she continued with her conversation exactly where she had left off. Lady Hermione feigned illness and made a hasty departure.

Another amusing incident involving Horace occurred one sultry summer's day. An engineer was summoned to the manor house to repair a malfunctioning telephone—Dottie's life support system. While the engineer was working in the kitchen, Dottie entered, smiled her seductive smile and whispered, "Would Horace like to come to bed with Mummy for a while?" The engineer turned the color of an over-ripe tomato and began tripping on his feet as he tried to back out of the room. Dottie brushed past the tongue-tied gentleman and walked to the window sill where Horace was nibbling on a tulip. She scooped her favored pet, placed him on her shoulder, and sauntered back toward an even more bewildered telephone engineer.

"That was right funny ma'm," he nervously mumbled. "You see, *my* name is Horace." Dottie then introduced Horace the rat to Horace the telephone engineer and swept upstairs for her customary afternoon nap—not quite getting the joke.

Covington Court had been built on the grounds of an old convent which was destroyed during the dissolution of the Catholic Church. During the sixteenth century Henry VIII conveniently changed the official religion of England from Catholic to Protestant so he could divorce

Catherine of Aragon and marry his mistress Anne Boleyn. When the convent was destroyed, the nuns had been stripped, raped, and murdered by the King's soldiers. The violent means by which they met their maker had apparently trapped the nuns' spirits. On several occasions while I was working at the estate, weekend guests described sightings of nuns wandering through the maze and candles lighting and extinguishing without cause.

Covington Court, like all good English manor homes, had its share of ghost stories. I never placed much stock in them until the evening Dottie and I encountered Madelyne. Legend had it that in the early 1600s a beautiful young maiden named Madelyne married an older man who mistreated her. He knew she had only married him to please her father. Madelyn loved a dashing young man named Henry. They devised a secret plan to elope even though it would shame Madelyne and her family. Henry would rescue her in the small hours of the morning; a coach and two horses would be waiting by the garden gate. The lovers planned to go to France and live happily ever after.

On the designated evening Madelyne hid by the gate with a small bag. Her jealous husband, however, had discovered the plan and, unbeknownst to the young couple, was also waiting for the coach. He shot and killed Henry and locked Madelyne in the attic. Beside herself with anguish, Madelyne hanged herself with a petticoat. And ever since that horrible night, Madelyne's ghost roamed the grounds of Covington Court trying to find the spirit of her dead love.

Many guests reported hearing what sounded like the rustling of long silken skirts along the flagstone hallways late at night. Several times when I was living on the estate the heavy oak garden door would fly open and the alarms would ring (a large bolt secured this door so it was not easy for it to blow open). And then one very late evening Dottie and I heard someone sobbing in the rose garden. We decided to try and trace the source of the cries. Approaching the garden we heard a distinctively female voice cry out the name "Henry." As true Brits who delight in such fanciful legends, we took it all in our stride and decided to go to bed.

Richard was everything Dottie wasn't: rude, arrogant, and quite pretentious. His only redeeming feature was the number of zeros which followed the pound sign in his bank account. I could never understand how Dottie had wed and then lived with this particular man for so many years.

I was still working at Covington Court when their marriage finally came to an unhappy ending. The Sloans owned a cottage in the village; Richard decided to rent it to a Welsh woman named Sarah who said "ta" instead of "thank you," which in England is considered to be low-class slang. After a few weeks, rumors about Richard and Sarah began buzzing faster than a hummingbird's wings. In small villages everyone's business is scrutinized—especially those who live in the manor house (the largest house in the village).

The Lamb's Head, a local pub, was the social center of this quaint picture-postcard town. One of the most popular topics of conversation was the frequency with which Richard's black Jaguar was parked outside of Sarah's cottage. Richard was too arrogant to think anyone would

51

notice what he was doing. Poor Dottie, of course, was the last to know.

Richard took frequent business trips abroad; after twenty years of marriage, Dottie was not interested in accompanying her husband on every trip. She once told me, in fact, that she enjoyed the quiet while he was away. During one of his "business" trips to Paris, Richard and Dottie's prize stud took ill. Dottie telephoned her husband's hotel and asked to be connected to Mr. Sloan's room.

"I'm sorry madam," the operator replied, "Mr. Sloan is not available. But *Mrs.* Sloan is in the room if you wish to speak with her."

Dottie was shocked, to say the least. Despite the fact that her husband's affair was common knowledge, she knew nothing. Dottie didn't frequent The Lamb's Head, and the pub crowd was not about to come knocking on the door of the manor house. I was the only person who might have told her, but I make it a practice never to pass along such information unless I am specifically questioned.

Dottie caught her breath and asked if she could speak to Mrs. Sloan. When Sarah answered in her easily recognizable Welsh twang Dottie immediately hung up.

Like any sensible woman who believes her husband is having an affair, Dottie decided to have Richard investigated. She discreetly enlisted the help of a high-ranking government official who had always held a soft spot in his heart for Dottie. His investigation revealed that the Paris trip was only one of many such vacations Richard and his mistress had enjoyed together.

Dottie next confronted me with her findings and, at

that point, I had no reason to lie to her. I answered her questions and told her what I knew. She was hurt to learn that her husband's affair was common knowledge and that Sarah had stayed at the manor on several occasions when Dottie was in London (Sarah was snuck in through the garden gate at night).

A bitter divorce battle ensued; Richard showed no remorse. He threatened to transfer his assets out of the country unless Dottie agreed to settle for what *he* felt was a reasonable amount. After paying a small fortune in lawyer's fees, the Sloans were finally granted the divorce. Dottie kept the manor house and received a cash settlement, but it wasn't much considering she had played the perfect wife, mother, and hostess for twenty years. And to aggravate matters even more, it was Dottie's influential friends who had played a significant part in her husband's financial success.

Shortly after the divorce was finalized, Richard married Sarah, moved one hundred miles away, and started another family. Then, like a post-script to a morality tale, he was diagnosed with cancer. Richard lost a leg as well as many friends who stood by Dottie.

While working for the Sloans, I was called upon to arrange a major society wedding. The celebration was to be held on the grounds of Lady Lavistock's estate in a tiny hamlet in the Cotswolds. Her grand Elizabethan home was to be the splendid setting for a late June wedding. Two hundred hand-picked members of British society were invited to witness the marriage between Lady Lavistock's seventeen-year-old daughter Georgia and an eighteen-year-old Italian royal. Prince Carlo was the

53

handsome son of a European actress and an aging prince. The fact that Georgia was five months pregnant and had to be creatively attired in a loose-fitting white-and-pink gown was never mentioned by anyone. At least not on the actual wedding day. But several weeks later, predicting Georgia's delivery date became a popular topic of conversation during fashionable dinner parties.

Lady Lavistock, eager to please her pregnant daughter, decided on an elaborate and lavishly orchestrated wedding. I spent several weeks meeting with her to review all of the arrangements for the grand fête. Unlike most of my clients, Lady Lavistock had a very definite idea of what she wanted. The service took place in the local church with a great deal of pomp and circumstance. All of the invited guests gawked at the extravagance of the exceedingly billowy gown, the seemingly endless train and the hundreds of cream and pink roses which appeared to coat the entire surface of the church.

After the ceremony the guests were escorted to a line of Bentleys waiting to transport them to Lady Lavistock's idea of a fantasy wedding. As per her instructions, I had covered and tented the Olympic-size swimming pool for dancing, and surrounded it with trellises blanketed in rosevines, clematis, and passion flowers. Adjoining this was a very traditional U-shaped arrangement of banquet tables tented in peach canvas and covered in white and peach roses. The menu consisted of an assortment of hors d'oeuvres, watercress soup, cold poached salmon, poulet Vallé d'Auge (chicken with apples and celery cooked in Calvados), courgettes, baby new potatoes with mint, chocolate mousse with strawberries, Waldorf salad, and a multi-tiered wedding cake (traditionally fruitcake with marzipan).

It was fascinating to watch the guests intermingle. The bride's side of the family had invited an assortment of conservative, reserved, and stereotypically stuffy Brits; the groom was represented by southern Italians who could easily have been extras in Fellini's *8½*. They must have originated the word "celebration"; even the elderly widows dressed in black appeared to be having a (respectably) good time. In addition to the odd blending of English and Italian, the mixture of Georgia and Carlo's contemporaries with their parents' friends pulled the reception in wildly different directions.

All went well until the string quartet took their mid-evening break. Georgia, urged on by a few of her friends who probably thought Vivaldi was a new salad dressing, played disco music via the stereo system in the cabana. Those who had not been waltzing their way through the evening made a dash for the dance floor and began moving in a manner most English people can only fantasize about. During this musical transition one of Carlo's cousins had the idea to go for a bit of "slap and tickle" with one of the other guests in an adjoining field. Unfortunately, he forgot to latch the gate behind him. A dozen frisky and mischievous bullocks charged in to join the celebration. Suddenly everyone, including the bullocks, began running in all directions. Amidst the chaos, a section of the flooring over the pool gave way; while K.C. and the Sunshine Band continued singing "That's the way, uh-huh, uh-huh, I like it," a few of the younger guests danced their way below water level.

Lady Lavistock was horrified; she looked to me for

some immediate action. I quickly summoned several farmhands who lived on the estate. They rounded up the bullocks while I passed around smelling salts to a few semi-conscious women. I then tried to salvage the evening by supplying dry towels for the wet guests and unlimited drinks for the dry guests. Just as the party was beginning to recover, the young couple who had forgotten to latch the gate ran back to the reception area half-dressed. They had been rudely interrupted in the midst of their grand passion by the bullocks returning to the field. Everyone had a good laugh. Other than some disheveled guests and a few breakages, nothing serious had occurred to permanently mar the festivities. A few months later, the same group assembled to celebrate the christening of (what the press was told was) a remarkably premature baby.

Georgia and Carlo's marriage got off to a bad start—even after Lady Lavistock set them up with a London townhouse, a staff of five, three automobiles, and the nanny who had cared for both Lady Lavistock and Georgia. (The English are infamous for trotting old nannies out of the closet at the appropriate time. Most respectable families have at least one tucked away in the attic.) Although Nanny was quite elderly, she was very experienced and devoted to both Georgia and her newborn son.

My London flat was a mere stone's throw away from the newlyweds. I often visited Georgia during the week. We had lunch or took walks in the park together. Carlo was frequently away, trying to break into the film business. Because they were young, immature, and extremely spoiled, Georgia and Carlo had a difficult time making their marriage work. Their quarrels were legendary in my otherwise peaceful neighborhood. The young prince was insatiably possessive and jealous. He continually accused his young wife of infidelity and could easily become enraged if she wasn't home when he telephoned. Sadly, the prince's abuse eventually became physical. Georgia was ashamed to confide in anyone, but the bruises on her face revealed what she couldn't.

One very late evening someone began pounding on the door to my townhouse, screaming for help. I opened the front door and was startled to discover Georgia in a torn dress, looking beaten and somewhat bloody. I escorted her up to my second-floor flat and gave her a stiff drink— the British remedy (second only to tea) for every ailment. Once Georgia felt safely ensconced she began recounting the horrors of the awful row she had just had with her husband. She then telephoned her mother and Nanny in Wiltshire, where her baby was at the time. Lady Lavistock was shocked and furious; she tried to offer sound advice which only instigated a shouting match.

After a long and heated discussion they finally decided that Georgia should remain in my apartment until her mother arrived to sort things out. Moments later my intercom began buzzing non-stop. An hysterical person was screaming that he knew Georgia was inside and demanded to speak to her. I denied her presence but to no avail. I wanted to telephone the police at once but Georgia begged me not to. The British are ever conscious of scandal; the papers would have feasted on this particular story for weeks. After Georgia began crying I agreed not to telephone the authorities. I lived on the second floor of a townhouse and felt reasonably secure. Georgia accompanied me into the kitchen, where we brewed a pot of tea. Meanwhile, the Prince stood in the street of my fashionable private mews, screaming obscenities and threatening Georgia and myself with violence. Every neighbor within a two-block radius was hanging from his window or balcony to watch the show. The Prince suddenly pulled out a pistol and began wildly waving it through the air. This lessened the crowd's interest considerably, and they quickly disappeared. Like a madman the Prince began climbing the trellis to my garden terrace. Something had to be done. In an authoritative voice, I instructed a very hysterical Georgia to stop crying and help me pull the shutters over the windows. We then pushed an armoir in front of the shutters to block his potential entry.

The Prince reached the balcony and began pounding on the glass, breaking several panes and cutting his hands. The only calming element to this scene was the sound of distant sirens which gradually increased in volume. Georgia and I locked ourselves in my bedroom closet just as the police arrived. The Prince was apprehended and taken to prison. Through the help of influential friends (the owner of one of London's leading papers was an admirer of Lady Lavistock), the entire incident escaped mention in the press and the charges were dropped. Lady Lavistock had the marriage quietly terminated; she sent Georgia, nanny, and child to a rented villa in France for three months until the entire episode became a blur.

For months I received the most disconcerting looks from my very conservative neighbors, which I chose to ignore. I did, however, install a very complex alarm system in my flat. The Prince moved to America and eventually became successful in the film business.

Ironically, four years after the horrifying incident, Georgia and her impassioned Italian met again, remarried, and to this day, appear to be (peacefully) happy.

One of the loveliest individuals I had the pleasure to be associated with during this period was a woman named Lady Cordelia Ottoline. She was, during her youth, one of the most sought-after models in Europe and had been photographed on more occasions than she could remember. Cordelia was a legend of her time whose beauty, charm, sophistication, and wit had captured the hearts of royalty and most of Europe's wealthiest eligible gentlemen.

When I met Cordelia in 1972 she was married to Lord Peter Ottoline. Cordelia was an avid party giver and goer which is how our paths originally crossed—on the English social circuit. Her husband Lord Peter and she had been friends for twenty-five years before they married. How they happened to marry after a quarter-century of friendship is quite an unusual story.

Cordelia's closest childhood friend was a woman named Yvonne who, at nineteen, had married Lord Peter Ottoline, the titled son of a wealthy north country landowner. As the years went by, Yvonne's marriage took on an air of boredom. Lord Peter was a perfect gentleman but he and Yvonne were a mismatch. Cordelia, also married, lived on a large estate near Ottoline Hall. The two couples frequently socialized and were all close friends.

Yvonne eventually met a handsome gentleman and embarked on an affair which, unbeknownst to Lord Peter, went on for a number of years. During that period Cordelia's husband died in a car crash and she decided to end her highly successful modeling career. When Yvonne reached her thirty-fifth birthday she decided she wanted a divorce so she could marry her lover. Because divorces are not quite so simple to secure in Britain, Yvonne devised a plan to ensure her success. She suggested that her husband and her best friend run off together and stay in a hotel. Yvonne would hire a private detective to follow them and gather the necessary evidence. Yvonne would then be able to get her divorce on the grounds of Lord Peter's desertion and adultery; she would maintain her dignity—a very important requirement in British society. As a gentleman who only wished his wife the best, Lord Peter was willing to go along with the plan. Cordelia didn't mind because Yvonne was her best friend and it was agreed that she wouldn't be named in the divorce papers.

After all the arrangements had been made Lord Peter and Cordelia checked into a lovely Brighton hotel to pretend they were in the midst of a wildly passionate affair. The private detective followed and questioned the proprietress about her two romantic guests. Shortly after the detective left, the proprietress knocked on the door to the supposedly adulterous suite and, upon receiving permission, popped her head in.

"You don't have to worry. I didn't tell 'em nothin, luv. You're both safe 'ere. So nice and polite. My, what a lovely couple you'll make."

She left as quickly as she had appeared. Lord Peter and Cordelia fell about laughing: their carefully laid plan had been ruined.

After several months, Yvonne was eventually successful in securing a divorce. And Peter and Cordelia's friendship developed into a loving relationship which culminated in their marriage. Yvonne's beau, unfortunately, refused to marry her. This left Yvonne as the "odd man out" and put a strain on her friendship with Cordelia. But Cordelia always says, "I married my best friend."

I acted as host/party planner for several social functions at the Ottolines' 300-acre estate. Ottoline Hall was a Georgian masterpiece, one of the top ten grade-listed buildings in Bath. In England, certain historical buildings of architectural merit are graded either 1, 2, or 3. Like landmarked buildings, they cannot be destroyed.

Once when Lord Peter was away, Lady Cordelia gave a dinner party. One of her guests included a very straight-laced, ex-Rowdene school marm. The elegant party took a turn for the worse when one of the guests, a lady of high social title, was in the midst of a very involved story. When she reached the climax her high-pitched shrill voice broke through all other conversation.

"I told them to just piss awwhhhhf!" she shrieked with delight. "Be awwhhhhf my estate before I have your goolies cut awwhhhf and made into a vinaigrette salad!!"

The prim and proper school marm clutched her pearls and almost choked in shock at such language. Then to make matters worse, one of the gentleman got slightly tipsy. When the main course was served, he poked at his food and, after learning it was lamb's tongue, screamed, "I never eat offal!" To which the shrill-voiced lady retorted, "No, but you slept with it for fifteen years!" referring to his recently divorced wife whom she had always disliked. Lady Cordelia, ever the perfect hostess, suggested retiring to the conservatory for a musical recital as soon as possible.

Lady Cordelia and I quickly became friends. She was a fun-loving person who was always game for a lark. One particular day we were having drinks, discussing a very disturbing recent event. Two very valuable Georgian urns had disappeared (plants included) from the entrance to my home. They had been spotted outside a cottage in a neighboring village. The "thief" was a former friend who had acted out of peevishness—not necessity. We devised a plan to rectify this situation.

Lady Cordelia and I, fortified with Dutch courage (several gin and tonics) climbed into her Land-Rover and sped to the perpetrator's cottage. After ascertaining no one was in residence, we huffed and we puffed as we quickly lugged the antique urns into the get-away vehicle. Always the polite souls, we left a note which stated, "Sorry to have missed you. The urns have been transported back to their original owner."

My days as a caterer and part-time majordomo were filled with fun and adventure. I loved the diversity of experience and all of the wonderfully wild and exotic people I met. But the time was approaching where I felt ready for a long-term project. Fortunately I would not have to look very far or wait very long.

Five

By the end of 1972 I had logged thousands of miles commuting between London and the West country. My professional life was centered in and around Bath, overseeing two businesses and serving a multitude of catering clients. My private life, however, gravitated toward the magnetic attraction of the big city. London's limitless selection of restaurants, theatres, discotheques, and nightclubs was irresistibly tantalizing to an adventure-loving twenty-year-old. While New Yorkers were hustling the night away at fashionable clubs, the English were not far behind. I danced into the other side of midnight at Regine's and Yours or Mine on Kensington High Street. When the records stopped spinning at 4 A.M. I frequented after-hours clubs where entrance was by membership only. Discreetly tucked away at the tops of winding staircases in back alleys, these private establishments lured a collection of characters celebrating every possible social, sexual, and psychological deviation. Compared to the black-and-white existence of my weekends in the country, my life in London was like living in a David Hockney painting.

By the following spring, I felt my energies dissipating; it was time to focus on one particular employer or business. Neither the restaurant in Bath nor the majordomo position at Covington Court was sufficiently stimulating to warrant a full-time commitment. Deciding to pursue life's possibilities in the big city, I sold the restaurant and take-away business (along with my house in Wiltshire) and gracefully parted company with Dottie Sloan. At the time I had every intention of making London my permanent home. Fate, however, sometimes unexpectedly intervenes, gently nudging us in an equally unexpected direction.

Shortly after I made my decision to base myself in London I accepted an invitation from my mother to vacation with her in the south of France. She booked a suite at the Hotel Negresco in Nice, an opulent if somewhat camp structure, infamous for its gold and purple lobby filled with black nubian statues. During our afternoon tea at Queenies we ran into M.S., a family friend, who asked us to join him for dinner. Four hours later, we were seated at Moulin de Mougin, a famous French restaurant noted for its raspberry soufflé.

During dessert, M.S. asked what I had been doing to occupy myself. I provided him with a brief summary of my various business endeavors, which suddenly prompted him to offer me a job. M.S. wanted me to accompany him to Europe for the summer and manage his villas in Boully-sur-Mer on the French Riveria, and Forte de Marmi on the Italian Riviera. His unexpected offer established a pattern which would follow me for years: I never had to look very far for a unique employment opportunity—the opportunities, in fact, came looking for me. Although working for M.S. was a diversion from my London plans I was so excited by the idea that I almost dropped my soufflé spoon. At the time, M.S. was one of the richest men in England and somewhat of a ladies' man; he knew everyone who was "anyone." A jet-set summer with the wealthy European playboy would definitely be a once in a lifetime experience. I enthusiastically accepted M.S.'s offer and became a full-time major-domo.

Although I had been exposed to many affluent and aristocratic families, M.S. was in a class of his own. He was an entrepreneur. While the landed gentry were playing polo and hunting in the fields, M.S. was in the boardroom making multi-million-dollar deals. He had inherited a vast sum of money during the war which he rapidly multiplied by investing in real estate and desalination plants in Arabia. His family, prominent European aristocrats, were murdered during the Second World War; their home and possessions were confiscated. Shortly before the Nazis occupied Eastern Europe, M.S. and the family fortune had been transported to Switzerland for safekeeping. Sadly, he was the only member of his family to survive. Over the next forty years M.S. gradually bought back many of his family's possessions whenever they surfaced at auction. In Geneva, I once watched him bid on his family's monogrammed silver which he hadn't seen for over thirty years. There was no way to prove it had been stolen. I later learned that the once stately family residence had been converted into a bus station.

When I began working for M.S., he was in his early sixties, divorced from a European movie star and living the life of a bachelor. In addition to two European villas, he owned a large mansion in Westminster, an estate near Ascot, a fleet of Bentley sports cars and the magnificent 130-foot yacht *Sole e Luna* (sun and moon). He traveled extensively for both business and pleasure and lived his life with an enormous passion and enthusiasm—an approach I wholeheartedly supported. Despite an extravagant life-style he was always in control of his financial affairs.

M.S. was well known for two characteristics: He spoke ten languages fluently and his wardrobe, consisting of only three colors (black, navy blue, and white), was duplicated in each of his residences. When shopping for clothes I purchased five of everything: one each for London, Ascot, Italy, France, and the yacht. I found his approach to wardrobe planning quite sensible; it certainly simplified the usually unpleasant task of packing and unpacking whenever we traveled.

M.S. gave me carte blanche to organize and manage everything pertaining to his social and private lives. Not surprisingly, as summer slipped into fall I was only too happy to continue my association with him. During one three-month period we journeyed to Venice, Florence, Paris, Geneva, St. Moritz, and Athens, where I watched him buy a fleet of cargo ships one week and sell them a few days later for a large profit. Everything was first class—cars, planes, hotels, restaurants, and clubs—a non-stop whirlwind of activity I thoroughly enjoyed.

* * *

M.S. had a penchant for multiple quantities of the very best life had to offer—including beautiful young women. It eventually became part of my job to manage this exceedingly personal aspect of his life—to boldly go where (I presumed) no majordomo had gone before. Nothing in my background had prepared me; there were no chapters in the unofficial guide book for majordomos titled: "How to Fulfill the Sexual Requirements of Your Employer" or "Procurement or Productivity: How to Know Which Is Which." I soon realized I would have to write this particular chapter on my own.

I was initially surprised but not embarrassed by M.S.'s request. Although this was the first time I had been asked to perform such duties for an employer it certainly would not be the last. What became interesting to watch in the years to come was the way in which future employers approached the topic. Some brought up the general subject of sexuality to see how I would react. One gentleman once left a note on his breakfast tray requesting assistance. M.S., however, was very direct. He stated his preference for uncomplicated sex which he defined as "a generally good time with no expectations or emotional commitments." Perhaps the ten-year marriage had permanently fulfilled his need for long-term relationships. He preferred entertaining and traveling in the company of six to ten stunning women at any given moment.

Once I agreed to accept the special assignment, I attempted to locate suitable candidates through my many social contacts. These were not street types or prostitutes in the conventional sense of the word. Some were models from Europe's finest magazines; others were young socialites who wished to capitalize on their assets. All were handsomely paid to be "guests" (which is how they were always described) at M.S.'s dinner parties. Many had such a good time they became regular fixtures.

The "guests" were invited to a particular function to entertain high-powered businessmen from all over the globe. If we were expecting eight men for dinner I would invite eight stunning guests and assign each to a specific gentleman. The women were paid handsomely (usually five hundred pounds) merely to show up. The only requirements were that they arrive beautifully coiffed and dressed and that they made every attempt to inflate the size of the businessmen's egos. If, during the course of the evening, they inadvertently inflated something else, I was never a witness. It wasn't a difficult assignment: most of the men already had highly developed opinions of themselves. They regarded any compliments tossed their way as an affirmation of what they already knew. The ladies were well-educated and multi-lingual; they could intelligently discuss such subjects as art, politics, opera, literature, and theatre. What, if anything, they did *after* dinner (and how much they negotiated) was none of my business.

The women adored M.S. He was sophisticated, cultured, generous, polite, and exceedingly well-mannered. He stood whenever the ladies entered or exited a room and fussed over their every comfort. If one of them didn't have a suitable dress for a particular party he would send the distraught creature to Harrods in London or to one of the exclusive St. Germain boutiques in Paris to purchase whatever she needed. He wanted the women to be beautiful and happy.

M.S. was obsessed with beauty. His homes, automobiles, and yachts were exquisite—every detail was perfection itself. Heads turned whenever he stepped off the Italian cruiser in some jet-set harbor surrounded by his collection of fetching females. I became very good friends with one of the regulars. Katerina was a vivacious and voluptuous blonde from Munich who knew how to put her best assets forward. Once, while we were engaged in a private conversation during a dinner party, I asked Katerina how she really felt about her work. She raised two perfectly plucked eyebrows and quickly glanced around the room to see if anyone was looking. After taking me by the hand and pulling me to a corner where we wouldn't be overheard, Katerina leaned into me as if she was going to whisper something in my ear.

"I loooove itttt!!!!" she screamed while she shimmied her curvaceous body, attracting the attention of not only everyone in the room but, I'm certain, the entire neighborhood.

I got the point.

Katerina explained that she used to be a secretary but decided that life as a "lady" was far more lucrative.

"Let me tell you something, Desi-darling" (her nickname for me), "I slaved over forty hours a week typing some miserable pig's letters. I barely made enough to buy a new dress every few months. I was sick of being ogled and propositioned by some old lech. I thought if that's what they want they may as well pay for it! I'm not ashamed or embarrassed. Why not do work you enjoy? If I want a three-thousand-pound Chanel suit I buy it. If I need a two-month vacation I take it! Listen darling, Katerina knows: Self-employment is the only way. These wives and mistresses that trade their independence for less than I make in a week can have it! I'm not taken for granted, abused, or neglected. So you tell me who has the better deal?!'' she concluded as she flashed an enormous emerald ring in my face.

Katerina made such a strong case for her chosen profession that I was ready to sign up and start working immediately. One of her clients was an Arabian prince who gave her £2,000 to vacation with him every fourth weekend of the month—and that was just to show up—anything else was extra. He showered her with expensive trinkets, sent a private 747 to retrieve his weekend date, and never questioned Katerina about her activities when she wasn't with him. Many of the women I met worked in this fashion. They felt that being kept in the traditional sense was old fashioned; they fiercely guarded their independence.

I once took Katerina to a formal party in Bath. She provoked jealousy in both men and women: the ladies envied her poise, beauty, and style, not to mention the amount of attention she received from their husbands; the gentlemen took one look at their dowdy, dour-faced wives and wondered what my secret was to rate such a beauty. Katerina permanently retired in 1985 with a sizable bank account. She is currently married to a multimillionaire who knows nothing about her background. I am, of course, sworn to secrecy as to her new identity. We still visit each other on occasion and laugh about the good old days.

M.S.'s Italian piazza in Forte de Marmi was an architectural masterpiece, sculpted in white marble with statues, pools, and fountains. We usually moored his large yacht (which had a ninety-mph speed boat on board) up the coast at La Spezia—Forte de Marmi didn't have a harbor. We frequently took our guests to Portevenere to luncheon, where we would moor next to multi-million-dollar yachts whose owners were all plying for a table at a famous fish restaurant. Fortunately, M.S.'s best friend owned the establishment; we were always treated like visiting royalty.

No matter how wealthy M.S.'s friends were, they always treated me with kindness and respect. I'm certain they were following the example that M.S. set for himself. He regarded me as an equal and never used his power or position as a weapon. I was his right hand and confidant, handling all money matters which related to running his houses and yachts; I managed the staff and crew, who were always there for him because he treated them with respect and helped them if they were in trouble. M.S. exemplified the best qualities one could hope for in an employer and, as a result, he had happy and hard-working employees.

One of the greatest mishaps during my tenure with M.S. occurred in Greece. *Sole e Luna* was moored in Mykonos awaiting the embarkation of some businessmen and several "guests." The ladies were arriving on a private plane via Athens; the men were expected on a separately chartered 727 coming from London. The crew was busy readying the yacht for our departure. M.S., myself, and two of his pals had been on Mykonos for four days investigating a potential business deal. Once everyone arrived and settled into their respective state rooms we upped anchor and sailed away.

The guests were having a wonderful time, sunning and swimming by day, feasting and frolicking by night. M.S. and his crowd liked an occasional marijuana cigarette after dinner. The sights and smells of illegal substances were not unusual. (Hard drugs, pills, and cocaine were not popular in the mid-seventies with this particular set.)

After a few days of cruising the Greek islands, one of the businessmen (the chairman of one of London's largest merchant banks) and two of the ladies had to return to London. A private jet sped them to Athens for a connection. At the airport, customs examined their luggage and found two marijuana cigarettes stashed into the cigarette case of one of the women. They promptly placed her under arrest and carted her away. Drugs of any kind are frowned upon in Greece; marijuana possession is a serious violation of the law. The merchant banker radioed M.S., informing him that their friend had been arrested. She told the customs officials that she had been a guest on *Sole e Luna;* according to her, the drugs must have been placed in her cigarette case without her knowledge. (The silly cow was pinching them, of course.) It was only a matter of minutes before the authorities would be contacting M.S.

A half hour later we received the dreaded call. The coast guard ordered us to dock at the nearest port so they could search the boat. M.S. was absolutely livid; he instructed the ship's communications officer to switch the radio off. If we complied with the coast guard's request they would impound and search the yacht, causing untold damage and delay—not to mention the bad publicity. The staff and crew were put on immediate alert. All illegal substances were thrown overboard posthaste.

We had to plan a quick get-away. But how? If we took the yacht back through Greek waters it would surely be stopped. M.S.'s private jet had been grounded in Athens. There was only one way out. We were only two hours from Turkey so it was "full speed ahead" to the Turkish port. I quickly booked first-class flights from Istanbul to London. We arrived without further incident and flew directly to England. The yacht proceeded to Italy away from Greek waters.

In London, a team of powerful attorneys worked around the clock to resolve the crisis. After several weeks, the pot-pinching prisoner was released from jail and the jet was cleared to leave Athens. M.S. telephoned a few friends in the press in an attempt to prevent the story from becoming a major scandal—although mention of the incident briefly appeared in a tabloid.

The next week we were back in Italian waters preparing for a trip to the south of France. M.S. loved parties, and once or twice a week we would entertain up to seventy-five people in his home or on his yacht. The main ingredients were pulsating disco music, sexy sophisticated socialites, and an abundance of food, wine, and "weed." M.S. loved having crowds of people around.

One Christmas he invited everyone in his circle who was alone to join him for the holidays in Ascot. He bought everyone lavish presents, dressed as Santa Claus, and passed out the gifts. His regular group of "guests" were in attendance. I think they looked upon M.S. as an understanding friend who asked very little of them in return (and the pay wasn't bad). It wasn't really about sex; some women regularly attended his parties but never offered more than a kiss on the cheek. M.S. loved women more than anyone else I know. He respected their opinions and enjoyed their conversation as well as their beauty.

M.S.'s London townhouse was enormous and very chic. The third floor contained his private suite, complete with gym, sauna, sun-tan room (the machines were quite new at the time), multi-fauceted shower, jacuzzi, television room, and sleeping chamber with two baths—all decorated in beige and light wine—very popular in the seventies. The second floor included an equally lavish guest suite. The entire first level comprised the drawing room, which had floor-to-ceiling windows opening onto a walled garden area. The space could easily accommodate one hundred people for a party and often did. The sound system was the finest for its time, with control panels built into the walls of every room.

The staff quarters in the adjoining white brick carriage house were as beautifully decorated as the main house. Each bedroom was equipped with television, VCR, stereo, and private bath with balconies off of each double window. Although kitchens were traditionally in the basement, M.S. installed a state-of-the-art kitchen on the first level with views overlooking the garden. He felt his employees should have beautiful working conditions. A mini Cooper and two Jaguars were provided for the staff's use. Everyone ate as well as M.S. and received large bonuses and gifts at Christmas. They were entitled to four weeks' paid holiday, the opportunity to travel, and full life and health insurance with a pension plan. In the field of domestic employment, one is rarely provided with such benefits.

* * *

One of M.S.'s favorite indulgences was gambling. He regularly spun the roulette wheel at The Clairmont Club in London's Berkley Square as well as many European casinos. Like a true gentleman, he never complained about his losses. Sometimes, during a dinner party, he would impulsively decide to take the group for a bit of gambling fun. I usually organized the transportation, tables, drinks, and money. M.S. generous to a fault, would never invite his guests anywhere it might prove financially embarrassing. Since not everyone can afford to gamble, he provided the money. I would give each person an envelope containing twenty crisp new £100 bills from the safe. (I always kept at least £100,000 cash for emergencies or occasions such as this.) The ladies used to confide in me that they only pretended to gamble, saving most of the money. Champagne flowed endlessly until M.S. decided to push on to one of London's exciting discotheques. I enjoyed many such evenings dancing with Katerina at Annabel's—unless, of course, she was lavishing her undivided charm and attention on her assigned gentleman for the evening.

While gambling in Monte Carlo, in late 1974, M.S. and I met Contessa Giacovelli—one of the most stunning women I have ever seen. With raven hair neatly rolled into a pleat, she wore a black silk dress accessorized by a ruby and diamond choker with matching bracelet and earrings. Her grace and poise made it appear as if she stood still and the world moved around her. The moment M.S. saw her I knew he was mesmerized. She smiled and spoke to my employer in perfect social Italian; he invited her to join our group. La Contessa (which is how she was addressed) had an entourage consisting of four hand-some Italian men; one of the men was her brother. I later learned that although she was only thirty-two, she was one of the wealthiest women in Italy. She was born a Contessa, had married a British Earl and then an Italian, but now was divorced and free to enjoy her independence. She owned homes all over the world. La Contessa became a close member of our entourage for the next few months, and (although I had no idea at the time) she would eventually become my employer.

M.S.'s generosity and desire to help others knew no limits. One winter we rented a house in Barbados at St. James Beach, one of the most exclusive beaches on the island. The rental included the services of a housekeeper, a jolly black woman named Jean. It quickly became evident that the couple who owned the house had been over-working and under-paying this kindly woman. Apparently they felt rather shy about using such expressions as "please" and "thank you" but were quite demonstrative when it came to vocalizing their demands. M.S. was so impressed with the Jamaican woman's abilities and dismayed by the way she had been taken advantage of that he decided to take Jean and her young sons to London. Since Barbados is a member of the British Commonwealth, she had a British passport, so this was relatively uncomplicated.

Jean became housekeeper and part-time cook in M.S.'s Westminster townhouse. He loved her West Indian cooking, and her benevolent smile made you feel right at home. Jean always wore beautiful bright hats and dresses and was a wonderful addition to the staff. M.S. gave her a flat in his adjoining house and sent her boys to public school (which is private school in England).

Jean's figure was as big as her heart; she easily tipped the scales at three hundred pounds. One day she was climbing down a spiral staircase to the rubbish hut in the basement. Her massive frame got stuck. I wasn't quite sure whom to call for help but decided on a locksmith. He had to cut the staircase into pieces to free the somewhat embarrassed housekeeper. Immediately thereafter, I arranged to have a new staircase installed which was twice as wide.

Jean stayed with M.S. for over fourteen years, until she became ill and died of cancer. M.S. was like a father to Jean's sons, buying them whatever they needed, taking an active interest in their lives. He even attended all their school functions. When the elegantly dressed Englishman and the colorfully attired cook arrived at the exclusive boy's school in the Bentley, they certainly received their share of stares. What talk there was! Her boys, however, were well-educated and grew up to be successful. One is an attorney; the other, a director in an export company. Years later, by chance, I interviewed with the couple Jean had worked for in Barbados. They were extremely arrogant South Africans who not only had a primitive attitude regarding blacks but about domestic help in general.

In the winter of 1974, M.S. slightly modified his attitudes about relationships; he had a string of girlfriends who lived with him on an on-again, off-again basis. Shortly before Christmas he had a falling out with a high-strung lady named Helena and began dating a woman called

77

Allison. The ladies were unaware of each other's existence.

On New Year's Eve we had a large dinner party and were due to leave very early the next morning for Geneva. I stayed overnight in the guest suite, as I often did in such cases. At 2 A.M. I was awoken by blood-curdling screams intermingled with M.S.'s cry for help. I quickly donned a robe, grabbed a brass candlestick, and dashed to his suite. When I peeked through the slightly ajar door I witnessed Helena and Allison in the midst of a hair-pulling, skin-scratching, leg-locking wrestling match. My earnest attempt to separate them merely sent more articles of clothing, bed linens, and pillows flying in all directions. I finally managed to restrain a screaming and kicking Helena by pinning her to a chair. She was completely hysterical. M.S. slapped her across the face and asked me to get her a drink. She quickly downed a bourbon, which calmed her for a few seconds. But as soon as she saw Allison she recommenced her impression of a five-year-old throwing a temper tantrum. Allison, always obsessed with her appearance, was carefully examining her hair and face in the mirror.

I could see by the broken French windows that Helena had entered by a most unconventional route. She climbed up the trellis and swung her small frame onto the master balcony—a frightening feat considering the twenty-foot drop and the pointed fencing below. She might easily have been skewered on a spike.

Helena explained that she had been to a New Year's Eve party; after a few (most likely eight) whiskey sours, she became nostalgic for her romance with M.S. and decided a surprise visit was just the remedy for her post-relationship blues. When she spied Allison, however, her motivation changed from making-up to murder. While Helena was recounting her story I was still trying to deactivate the alarm system which M.S. triggered when he heard someone prowling about on the terrace. Sirens were shrieking, flood-lights flashing. Fortunately, our house had a reputation for loud parties at odd hours. Although we were surrounded by the foreign dignitaries of various embassies, no one ever called the police.

I drove Helena home while M.S. tried to calm a very shaken Allison. A large black eye darkened her enthusiasm for the impending trip. A doctor was called to make a post-night visit; the trip was canceled while we regrouped.

When Fabio, the butler, came on duty the next day, we told him someone had tried to break in, the alarms frightened the burglars, and Allison accidentally bumped into the bathroom door. Meanwhile, our security staff had all the windows and terrace doors replaced with shatterproof glass and, happily, nothing like this ever happened again.

Years later, Jean told me that she had heard the ruckus that night and was about to call the police. She crept into the house with a poker but recognized my voice and decided the situation was under control. We laughed and she said that a three-hundred-pound wigless black woman at 4 A.M. would scare anyone. She never mentioned anything the next day, as it would have embarrassed her employer.

M.S., an astute businessman who was almost as passionate about disco as I was, felt London needed a new "in" place. In the summer of 1975 he asked me to scout for potential locations. He proposed to invest whatever was necessary if I would agree to manage the club. I have always been stimulated by new projects and challenges which require research and imagination. M.S.'s idea was extremely exciting: it would allow me the opportunity to utilize many of my skills in conjunction with my love of music. I immediately began an exhaustive search for the perfect space.

After several weeks I discovered a location just off Bond Street in London's fashionable West End near the Embassy Club, Legends, Annabel's, and Mortimers—the playgrounds in which the rich and the restless revel into the small hours of the night. I took one look at a massive undeveloped basement space and envisioned what was to become one of London's hottest and sexiest nightclubs: Pacific Plaza.

Six

Pacific Plaza was the realization of an adolescent fantasy. I thought it would be decidedly decadent to transplant the bikini-clad bodies of Malibu Beach into London's lascivious night-life. I was confident the synergy of sand, sea, and sex would create an atmosphere encouraging patrons to let their inhibitions (and expenditures) run wild. Discotheques are like adult amusement parks: For twenty dollars you can abandon the dull, drab existence of everyday life and take a ride into the neon-lit world of unlimited possibilities. In the split-second pictures photographed by flashing strobe lights, no one is ugly; everyone is a star. M.S. thought that a successful club should be like a highly skilled hooker: both specializing in seduction, both capable of arousing the most uninspired partner. Bearing that in mind, I tried to create an irresistible lover.

Past a grand canopy extending from an otherwise ordinary building, beyond a dimly lit staircase descending into London's lower depths, the fantastical world of

Pacific Plaza began. In 1975, the combination discotheque/restaurant was unique: No one had previously created a club inspired by the beaches of California. Large umbrella tables and wicker chairs rested against a sky blue-and-white background. A thirty-foot wave realistically painted across an entire wall appeared as if it might crash into the tables at any moment. In the back, an elaborately lit dance floor enticed the eclectic crowds to "set themselves free," bumping and grinding to the very latest disco sounds.

My first choice for a hostess proved to be a social disaster. Sybil had that snooty edge which only we British possess. She frequently greeted the less glamorous customers with a look of disdain. During her job interview I stated that I was looking for a "Queen of the Night." Perhaps she had confused categories of royalty: Sybil behaved like a spoiled princess.

A hostess is the first person a patron encounters. An engaging smile or a seductive laugh can often persuade the most boring financier to change his focus from two-dimensional figures to the three-dimensional type. Pacific Plaza needed a tantalizing temptress—a wild and sexy dynamo in a slinky dress who could play part-time traffic controller and full-time diva. After weeks of interviews, the closest example I found was a thirty-eight-year old woman from Liverpool who had once belly-danced for the Beatles. I was despondent but not discouraged.

One dreary London day, while I was seated at the bar reviewing job applications, the gods of disco miraculously answered my prayers. Above the clatter of someone stacking glassware I heard a distinctively Midwestern voice.

"Are you Desmond?"

I swiveled on the bar stool and gasped when I located the source of the nasality: a five-foot-four-inch sexy apparition of fun wearing an abstract, form-fitting dress. As I paused for a moment to take in the full impact of the image I thought Picasso must have used her body for a canvas.

The energetic young woman hopped onto a neighboring bar stool and crossed two very perfect legs. "Do you have any jobs available?" she asked while twirling shoulder-length blond hair with a set of ruby red fingernails. Before I had a chance to answer she introduced herself as Lisa Martin from Iowa and proceeded to narrate her past experiences in a rapidly rolling voice.

Ms. Martin obviously knew how to take control of a situation. As she rattled on I didn't so much listen to what she was saying but took in her overall impression. Lisa embodied all of the qualities I was searching for in a hostess: beauty, energy, enthusiasm, wit, and that certain edge people have who are hungry for a new experience. During her monologue I ascertained that she had traveled the world for the past four years through a series of jobs and adventures. (A kindred soul, I thought to myself.) She loved disco, late nights, parties, unconventional people, and being in the middle of a social hurricane. Early twenties, single, no ties. Absolutely perfect! I hired her on the spot and she started that evening.

During my thirty-eight years I have been to a plethora of parties from Bangkok to Beverly Hills; never have I seen anyone work a room like Lisa. With quick, sharp movements, spinning from one person to the next, she made the most high-powered Hollywood agent look passive. Even when she stood in place (which wasn't often) she kept moving to the beat of the disco drum. One evening I escorted Lisa onto the dance floor; she began spinning and twirling throughout an entire song. I christened her "Girly-Whirly" on the spot and baptized her in champagne. That night a new star was born unto the London club scene.

Girly had unlimited energy (without the support of any chemical substances); her enthusiasm and charm were second to none. She instinctively knew how to arrange people to create an exciting atmosphere, prominently displaying the rich, royal, beautiful, and bizarre individuals at the most visible tables. Badly dressed, rude, or low-class types were hidden at obscure points around the perimeter of the room. Girly was super-toned and very slim; overweight people were her least favorite. Although I chastised her on several occasions she defended her position by stating that they blocked passage for seating and serving. Exceptions were always made for VIPs and pop stars—no matter how heavily they tipped the scales.

The male and female wait staff adored her. A waiter relies on a hostess' ability to fill his or her station, providing a continual flow of people throughout the night. Girly never let anyone down. She was charming but firm when necessary; she could see trouble before it arrived and always utilized the services of the bouncers to handle any unpleasant situations. I felt extremely fortunate to have her as an employee.

The staff dressed in tight white satin shorts, blue and pink T-shirts which blazed "Pacific Plaza," and roller skates—which quickly eliminated *many* potential employees. Most were blond-haired, blue-eyed Americans in their twenties who had been hired for their Nautilus physiques as well as their ability to skate a tray full of drinks through a crowded club. We had "skater-waiter" classes twice a week to practice various techniques, learning the best way to avoid accidents. They were a wonderful group of hard-working individuals whose movie-star smiles and American accents charmed the crowds.

During the mid-seventies the art of public relations was not as highly developed as it is today. In the image-conscious nineties a personal publicist is second only to a personal trainer. From film stars to Fifth Avenue society matrons, everyone who wants to be "someone" is hiring one. I have even heard of publicists who hire publicists to help promote their services so they, in turn, can help promote. . . .

Promotion or product: which is more important? Ask any disappointed author, actress, or recording artist and he or she will describe the painful experience of being improperly promoted. Ask their respective companies and you might receive a brief description of the inadequacies of their client's latest vehicle. I have always believed that the manner in which something is sold is just as important as the product itself. Toward that end I hired two muscular young men who worked full-time promoting Pacific Plaza. Dressed in satin briefs and skin-tight T-shirts imprinted with the club's name, they skated through London's winding streets distributing invitations—and attracting a great deal of attention. To help promote a special party, the entire staff skated through Hyde Park bearing trays of cocktails. This created quite a stir amongst London's conservative daytime society. Television news cameras arrived and filmed the event.

Thanks to the free commercial from the BBC we were soon inundated with hundreds of new faces who wanted to be a part of what everyone was talking about.

Pacific Plaza was always packed with an assortment of fun- and food-hungry individuals. The menu consisted of basic American fare: spinach salad, bacon-lettuce-tomato sandwiches, hamburgers, ribs, and barbecue chicken. We attracted a wide diversity of disco-maniacs. You never knew who you might literally bump into on the dance floor—a billionaire Arab prince or a shop assistant from Woolies (Woolworth's). M.S. and his entourage were frequent visitors whenever the party was in town. At the time I agreed to create and manage the club I relinquished many of my former duties. I no longer traveled with him but still supervised the various household staffs. All of M.S.'s "guests" flocked to "PP" (our nickname) with their beaus of the evening. They ordered expensive champagne or cocktails with such unorthodox names as "Hitler's Revenge" and "Her Majesty's Secret Elixir." Our chief bartender was a fiery Australian named Sally who was exceptionally creative at mixing drinks. For a time, Pacific Plaza was one of the hot spots of London's West End (along with Legends and The Embassy Club).

My friends, Prince Ali and Princess Ara Ramurshidabad, were PP regulars who always arrived dressed in fashionable evening attire. Although often mistaken for husband and wife, they were actually brother and sister—the last of the Bengal princes from Calcutta. The Princess wore the largest jewels I have ever seen—all real stones inherited from her family. The Ramurshidabads carried an air of royal sophistication and were always given a prominent table where everyone could gawk at the Princess's jewelry. Princess Ara was a five-foot-ten-inch beauty with jet-black hair and breathtaking carriage. She dressed in beautiful floor-length saris which made it appear as if she floated on air when she moved through a room. Her brother was tall, swarthy, and very handsome, with a predilection for mischief and practical jokes.

One night I was driving Ali and Ara home in my black mini Cooper which had the unfortunate registration of DYKE 265. It is quite common for the richest people in London to own a Bentley or Jaguar and have a mini as a run-about. Just as we were approaching their fashionable London square, a policeman flashed us down for speeding. While the gentleman waited for me to show him my license, Ali (who had consumed more than his fair share of champagne) indignantly proclaimed, "Do you know who I am!?! I am Prince Ali Ramurshidabad, the last of the Bengal princes!"

To which the policeman dryly retorted, "And I'm Queen Victoria's sister!"

Upon hearing this Ara (who also had been imbibing) extended a bejewelled hand and said, "Then we must be related. Why don't you join us for a drink?"

I once attended a glorious birthday party for Ara in the Ramurshidabad's immense Kensington flat. Housed in an entire floor of a large apartment building, it contained two enormous private suites. The communal entertaining rooms were decorated in exquisite silks, priceless rugs, and furnishings from around the world. The evening began with champagne, cocktails, and various hors d'oeuvres. Everyone was dressed in evening wear. Ara appeared in the most magnificent sari, her neck, ears, and wrist adorned with enormous pear-shaped emeralds and diamonds.

Dinner was announced at precisely 8 P.M. A gong sounded as two Indian butlers ceremoniously opened a pair of gilded doors, revealing a large room with crystal chandeliers and several tables surrounded by gold chairs with green silk cushions. The walls were draped and tented in autumn colored silks. The ambiance and decor transported me to the palaces of bygone days. One prominent guest from a noble Indian family told me the chamber was a copy of one of the Ramurshidabads' state rooms in India; most of the furnishings in their palatial apartment had been shipped to England when the family fled their native country. The nobleman assured me Princess Ara's jewelry for the evening was a mere sampling of what she owned; the large ruby she wore on her forehead was worth a king's ransom. I was mesmerized by the experience; it was one of the most magical, elegant evenings I have ever attended.

Late one evening a group of twelve solemn-looking men and women stormed into Pacific Plaza and asked for a table for twelve. They were obviously undercover police. Girly remained calm and cranked up the charm. She paused for a moment, reviewed the reservation sheet, and cooed, "I'm sure we can squeeze in such a handsome group. Follow me please." As soon as she led the way they flashed police badges and instructed her to turn the music off and the lights up. Thankfully it was midweek. But several nervous patrons requested their bills and made a hasty departure.

The police proceeded to methodically question the entire staff, specifically focusing on our operating hours. They raided the club because they believed we were in violation of our license. We were originally given a 2 A.M. closing time. I had recently applied and received a one-hour extension. Unfortunately, the English judicial system was backed-up due to a strike (our favorite national pastime) and I had not yet received the new permit. Of course no one had bothered to inform the police. They were so resolute in their investigation you would have thought we were conspiring to murder Her Majesty and the entire Royal Family. After a very long hour the group departed with a file full of notes. (They were later shown the new paperwork by the club's attorney and the case against us was dropped.)

We were all somewhat shaken by the intrusion so I asked everyone to join me in a glass of champagne.

"Where's Sally?" someone asked, looking for our Aussie bartender. No one had seen her since the arrival of the police. We checked the store room; her coat and purse were hanging on the wall. After a ten-minute search we discovered her in the walk-in refrigerator trying to warm herself between two sacks of potatoes. Sally explained that she ran into the cooler to hide from the police because she didn't have a work permit. The chef had seen the slightly ajar door and slammed it shut. The inside handle was broken, which made it impossible for Sally to free herself. She couldn't risk crying out for help because she didn't know if the police had left. Everyone laughed and said that they didn't have work permits either. Eighty percent of my staff were Americans in the same situation. I decided to defrost our embarrassed bartender with a drink. Girly flicked down the lights, pumped up the volume, and began twirling her way toward the dance floor. Everyone danced and drank until the police were just an unpleasant memory.

Girly and I had many larks together. One spring weekend Lord and Lady Simpson invited me to attend a smart luncheon at their country manor in Somerset. I decided to liven an otherwise stuffy weekend by taking Girly as my guest. When I introduced the aristocratic couple to London's hottest hostess the sides of their mouths pursed as if they had just sniffed the trace of an unpleasant odor. Perhaps the Simpsons were allergic to the smell of cowhide: Girly was exotically attired in a two-piece black leather outfit with fishnet stockings and four-inch pumps. I'm certain they thought she was a Soho dominatrix who practiced voodoo in her spare time.

Lady Simpson ignored Girly until the cocktail hour. She then made the rounds, asked her guests what they preferred to drink and received the usual replies: gin and tonic, whiskey straight . . . When she reached the corner of the garden where Girly and I were seated she stood very still, attempted a very sweet and sickly smile, and said, "What would you care for, Miss . . . Girly, I believe it was?"

Girly and I giggled, both knowing she would ask for her favorite beverage—very strong, very black coffee. As soon as Lady Simpson heard the request she began coughing uncontrollably and fled the garden. Girly's response had only strengthened Lady Simpson's conviction that this cow-clad coquette was part of some secret cult. Her forthright conversation, smattering of choice profanities to stress a point, use of slang and penchant for smoking at the luncheon table all combined to make Girly the talk of the party.

As I was preparing to leave I thanked Lady Simpson for her invitation.

"Desmond, dear," she began while incessantly patting my hand, "you know you're welcome here any time. But please, *please* leave these ill-mannered city creatures behind. Far be it from me to lecture you on suitable companions, my dear. But I just can't have them in my home. I'm sorry. It just won't do."

I smiled and reasserted what a lovely time we had.

Girly and I drove on to a grand country house hotel in Castle Coombe, one of those picture-postcard villages which wins awards each year as England's finest. We pulled up at the entrance, gave the Bentley to the valet, and marched inside in our leather gear (I was attired in leather pants and a black sweater). I requested a suite for the night only to receive looks of horror from the desk clerk as if we were gangsters on the lam. To calm the nervous gentleman I explained that we had just returned from an afternoon costume party in a neighboring village. He found the explanation odd but acceptable and showed us to a beautiful suite.

That evening we attended a fancy ball in Wiltshire at the home of one of my friends. Girly looked ravishing in a black lace and taffeta flamenco-styled gown. I wore the traditional DJ (dinner jacket), as we call them in England. The moment we arrived the aristocratic crowd began craning their necks like a group of anxious turkeys the day before Thanksgiving. Compared to the tweed- and wool-gowned country ladies, Girly looked like a Hollywood starlet. She was young, beautiful, sexy, and uninhibited—everything they weren't. I overheard a few of the guests comment that Girly was very "London in the country" (an English expression for overdressed) but she didn't give a fig. The men lusted after her firmly toned body, the women envied her every asset.

Throughout the night we danced and flirted; we were very wicked and out for fun. Much to our surprise, they began playing records during the orchestra's mid-evening break. Suddenly we heard the pulsating beat of the disco drum; we dashed to the dance floor, whirling, twirling, twisting, and turning. The crowd watched in amazement as we began performing the moves which earned Girly her name. Somehow, in the midst of our frenzy my cuff link caught Girly's dress and as I spun her around the floor the stitching came apart. While the Andrea True Connection sang, "More, more, more . . . How do you like it?" Girly's dress began unravelling, ripping away from her body. Caught up in the excitement of the dance, we were both unaware of what was happening. Not until we heard several cries and gasps did we see the lace piling up around Girly's feet.

The men began loosening their collar buttons due to a sudden case of overperspiration. We danced, undeterred, until Girly was twirling in black undies, suspenders, fishnet stockings and a silk slip. Such attire has been made fashionable due to the combined efforts of Madonna and Jean-Paul Gautier, but in 1976 it was quite shocking to a crowd of socialites who considered a naked elbow provocative. The dance ended to thunderous applause—mostly from the men who were salivating all over their black DJs. Girly unfastened herself from my cuff link and gathered her clothes. We dashed to the cloak room, retrieved our coats and laughed all the way back to our suite. Girly-Whirly was a marvelous character who contributed a great deal of fun and excitement wherever she went.

After two years of extremely hard work and rarely seeing the light of day (I usually got home by 8 A.M. and, hence, slept days) I was, once again, ready to move on. The life of the average club is short, to say the least; Pacific Plaza had reached its peak. M.S. and I were in agreement, and he sold the lease for a handsome profit.

During the previous six months M.S. had begun seriously dating an actress who was performing in one of those sex farces which, along with Agatha Christie's *Mousetrap,* seems to be many tourists' conception of British theatre. This particular woman had made such an impression on M.S. that he was redefining his attitudes about love, sex, and marriage. Much to the surprise of London society (M.S. being such a hedonist) they married in a very quiet ceremony after an eight-month courtship.

I continued an association with M.S. and his new wife for a brief period after their marriage. As events had taken an entirely new turn—he led a much quieter life—I began to feel bored with the job. M.S. entertained and traveled less frequently and, in certain respects, was becoming quite domesticated. His wife knew about his wild past— the parties, drugs, and "guests"—but she was very tolerant and understanding. Elizabeth was an intelligent woman who had seen the world; she knew jealousy would be the downfall of any relationship.

Although M.S.'s wife was adorable and charming, I preferred working for individuals as opposed to couples. New spouses can easily become jealous or feel threatened by the presence of a majordomo—someone who has spent more time with and has more intimate knowledge of their partners than they do. A new wife (or husband) may have a different approach to running a house and would feel more comfortable hiring someone new. During my grandparents' day couples did not divorce and remarry as easily as they do today; it was not unusual for a domestic to keep his position for twenty years or more. I could never be one of those types. I took a job and committed my life to it twenty-four hours a day. Because of the non-stop demands and the amount of myself I gave, by the end of a few years I would start to feel "burnt out," ready to move on to a new and exciting challenge. During my four years with M.S. I received many job offers wherever I went. Stealing good help is a favorite pastime amongst the rich and ready to be served.

I decided to place my professional life on hold for a few weeks and take a well-earned rest in Italy with Katerina. With me standing five-foot, nine-inches and my friend reaching almost six feet, we were a most striking couple who attracted our fair share of attention.

And as was frequently the case in my employment history, the next job fell into my lap.

Seven

While Katerina and I were sipping champagne in Portovenere we ran into Prince Rashid Al Fez Al, a young Arabian royal who had frequently patronized Pacific Plaza. During his many visits Prince Rashid and I had become quite friendly; he once invited me to a dinner party at his fashionable Mayfair townhouse, but I was unable to attend. Although a young man, the Prince was richer than rich, strikingly handsome, and a kind and fun-loving gentleman. He roamed the world with a jet-set crowd but never ventured more than five feet from two bodyguards and an aide de camp who took care of such trivialities as money. The Prince and his glamorous entourage were wild, wealthy, and wanton: they consumed cases of expensive champagne at Pacific Plaza's chosen tables and sometimes rose to a particular occasion by dancing on chairs. Each of the waiters begged Girly to seat Prince Rashid in his or her particular section: His bill for an evening easily exceeded a thousand pounds and he usually left a tip which equaled the bill. As a rule, I have observed that the level of one's generosity does not necessarily increase in proportion to the level of one's wealth, but the Prince always proved to be a most extravagant exception.

Prince Rashid invited Katerina and me to luncheon with him at Giuseppe's, a Portovenere restaurant famous for its preparation of fish. We chatted endlessly about our escapades at Pacific Plaza and the ever-changing London social scene. When I explained that the club had been sold and I was currently unemployed, the Prince's dark brown eyes flared with excitement; he whispered into the ear of his aide de camp, who abruptly fled the table. Katerina and I thought it odd but neither of us questioned the incident.

During dessert the aide de camp returned; he discreetly handed Prince Rashid a small package. Katerina and I exchanged a brief glance, wondering what the mystery was. Before we had a chance to give it a second thought the Prince suddenly grasped my hand, closed five quivering fingers around a small red box, and announced that he would be most honored if I would agree to work for him. He offered the present as a gesture of good faith. I opened the package, discovering an exquisitely hand-painted miniature porcelain globe. The Prince urged me to unfasten the clasp. The moment I lifted the Northern hemisphere a flash of green reflected the light of the blazing noonday sun. Gently resting against a cushion of white velvet was a magnificent 1.5 carat emerald stone. I was overwhelmed, to say the least. Prince Rashid explained that his aide was leaving to return to Paris. He needed someone who was free to travel for a year, organizing his social and private activities. He assured me that my life-style would equal his and insisted I name my own salary. It was not exactly your typical job interview.

I looked at Katerina, who was frantically nodding her head like some overwound mechanical doll. I surmised she felt I should take the job. Five seconds later I accepted the position (and the gift).

The job description sounded exactly like the type of work I had performed for M.S.—but on a more escalated scale. Although I didn't know it at the time, I would end up "organizing" the same aspect of Prince Rashid's private life that I had done for my Eastern European aristocrat. My new employer's "partners in passion," however, were of a slightly different persuasion: Prince Rashid preferred the amorous attention of men.

In the fall of 1976 we began our worldwide tour in Paris. The Prince's family owned an elaborately decorated apartment on the Avenue Foche, which he used whenever he was in town. After several days of packing and last-minute shopping, we boarded his private 727 and proceeded to conquer the social "hot spots" of the world. The Prince, like many Arabs, loved the Far East for its abundance of decadence and glamour. We jetted to Hong Kong, Singapore, and Bangkok, where boys are as plentiful as bowls of rice. The nightlife in Bangkok is the wildest in the world. Nearby Pattaya, a seaside resort on the gulf of Siam, provides an assortment of twenty-four-hour temptations. The downtown streets are lined with opium dens, pleasure palaces, and a surprisingly beautiful assortment of transvestites waiting to fulfill one's every fantasy (for a nominal fee, of course). I had never seen anything like it before. Many years later, for a lark,

I took my mother to one of the opium dens only to discover that she had already been there!

We always had enormous suites in the best hotels; everyone had adjoining rooms for security purposes. In addition to Prince Rashid, the bodyguards, and myself, our entourage consisted of a laundryman, secretary, valet, two pilots, and two stewards—all male, under forty, and very good-looking. Because of the size of our group, each arrival and departure was characterized by a mountainous procession of crocodile and Louis Vuitton luggage.

Gift-giving is an important part of Arab culture and, as I had learned during my "job interview," Prince Rashid proved to be a true Arab in this respect. I often felt like the proprietor of a duty-free shop, traveling with dozens of Cartier watches and lighters, Hermès scarves, and assorted jewelry and gems. In the event of a party, each guest had an exquisite memento next to his or her place card. Imagine arriving at the dinner table and discovering that instead of the usual smoked salmon your first course consisted of a gold Cartier Santos watch. I always sat with the invited guests unless a romantic dinner for two had been requested. But with the Prince's gregarious nature he preferred large numbers in everything he did. Whether traveling, eating, drinking, dancing or having sex, "the more the merrier" was the ruling philosophy. Most of his guests were various friends he had accumulated through traveling. Seldom, if ever, did he entertain family members.

September 1976 to August 1977 was to be Prince Rashid's year-long bachelor party—his last chance to run wild before returning to his homeland where he would marry and begin working for the family. It was estimated that the Prince's personal income exceeded $2 million a day (not counting cumulative interest from his vast holdings). Unlike many exceedingly wealthy people, he never mentioned money or asked the price of anything. He valued loyalty, trust, and honesty above all else. He was rarely rude to anyone and treated the staff members as if they were family. Although his brothers were dictatorial and rude, Prince Rashid benefited from a Western education, having attended schools in England, France, and Switzerland.

Also unlike many extremely wealthy people, the Prince truly lived at his income level. If he wanted something, he got it—no matter what the expense. At a moment's notice he would request a 150-foot yacht. It was my job to locate the required vessel and make certain it was staffed, supplied, and ready to sail. I frequently kept helicopters on call twenty-four hours a day at $1,000 per hour, and hired Lear jets and 727s to fly guests to and from our ever-changing locations. I chartered planes to fly to Persia to transport caviar for dinner parties and once (because nothing else was available) paid for the use of a 747 to bring an international jeweler from London to our current location (with a collection worth millions) so the Prince could select gifts for friends. Whenever we visited one of his many residences we were turban-deep in help; the ratio of staff to non-staff easily exceeded 5 to 1.

A majordomo is often part magician, part fairy godmother. Using all the tricks of his trade he must find a way to make his employer's every wish come true. Such a feat requires an amazing amount of knowledge, resourcefulness, imagination, and unending patience. I could easily spend three hours on the telephone trying to locate one particularly obscure item. If I didn't know where to find something, I had to find someone who did. It was like running through a maze trying to find the one necessary piece of information which would free me of the burdensome task. Some of the more unusual requests I have fulfilled include: procuring a pearl necklace at midnight in the middle of the Caribbean sea; organizing dinner for twenty with sixty minutes' notice; finding rare and out-of-season flowers to be shipped to remote locations; locating the appropriate individual to "bug" the home of a soon-to-be ex-wife to help secure custody of the children; placing a personal advertisement and reviewing the responses; furnishing an entire four-bedroom house (including everything from carpets to corkscrews) in three days; and pretending to be someone's boyfriend to make an inattentive lover jealous.

It was my job to fulfill Prince Rashid's every fantasy. He was, of course, exceedingly spoiled, but knew no other life; as demanding as he could be, he always maintained a sense of dignity in his requests. During my tenure with the Arabian royal he was never abusive or insulting.

For an entire year I had no private or social life other than my life with the Prince and his friends. He required around-the-clock attention. I didn't mind because I was young and exceedingly impressionable. My days (and nights) were filled with excitement and adventure—I never knew where we were going next.

Once, while flying over the Mediterranean, the pilot announced that we were passing over Malta. The Prince realized that he had never been to this particular group of islands; he instructed the pilot to land the plane and asked me to find suitable accommodations. I booked an entire floor of The Draganora Hotel, a large white structure perched on a cliff overlooking the water. We spent five days camped out at the hotel so the Prince could partake of his favorite pastime: gambling.

Our next stop was Jordan. People often ask me which country—out of the many I have visited—is my favorite. Jordan will always be one of those special places. I wore djellabas, rode camels, attended desert parties held in magnificently constructed tents, and snorkeled in the Red Sea, where beautiful coral reefs shimmered through clear waters in the relentless sun. I went on an archeological dig in Petra, a city carved into a mountainside dating back to Nabataean times. I was entertained in the gracious style of the Arabian culture. The people were polite, graceful, and hospitable, and they took me into their lives as one of their own. I drank a very thick, dark, and sweet type of coffee as frequently as I had consumed tea as a child. My time in Jordan had a very magical, mystical quality about it—perhaps because the culture was so different from any other place I had previously experienced.

We toured many of the Arab nations: Kuwait, Abu Dhabi, and Bahrain in the United Arab Emirates. I met a multitude of sheiks and princes and visited opulent palaces with spectacular furnishings and accessories. One gleaming white structure in the middle of a desert was surrounded by pink flamingos, a private zoo enclosed within a twenty-foot wall, and (with the help of a twenty-four-hour irrigation system) gardens as tropical as any in Florida.

The Prince and I had a great deal in common—especially an enthusiasm for shopping. Salespeople around the world salivated when they saw us pass through their doors. With the commissions they made during the Prince's brief visit they could vacation the rest of the year. Once, when I went car shopping with him in London, we purchased ten Rolls-Royce convertibles and four vintage Bentleys (one of which cost $300,000). All were equipped with every possible luxury, monogrammed with the family crest, painted the same color (white), and shipped to various locations throughout the world. This transaction was completed in twenty minutes and exceeded several million dollars.

At twenty-three, I loved the excitement of living at such an outrageously extravagant scale. There was a fairy-tale quality about my travels with the Prince which reminded me of the times Sarah and I used to play in Wentworth Park, making up stories about the indulgences of the very rich. I thought I had seen it all when I was working with M.S., but Prince Rashid approached another level entirely. We shopped for family, friends, and his many residences. In addition to the homes he already owned in London, Kent, Paris, Monte Carlo, Rome, and New York, he was building a large estate in Florida. Boxes were shipped daily from one place to another; it was my job to keep track of his purchases with the assistance of decorators and house managers—again, all male. Not a single woman worked in any position for the Prince although many socialized with him. This is not unusual for someone raised in male-dominated Arab society.

It was exhilarating to walk into designer men's shops

in Milan for a private showing; like my previous employer, Prince Rashid often purchased entire collections in triplicate for various homes. Even though he had a multi-seasonal travel wardrobe which grew larger by the day, he still maintained fully stocked closets in each city. One person per residence was assigned to oversee his vast wardrobe. They were usually elderly men who cared for the garments with amazing style. I was fascinated to watch Salib, our chief Pakistani valet, press a jacket. He would fill the sleeve with newspaper wrapped in tissue and methodically press each area to perfection, often working for one hour on a $20,000 jacket from Bijan. Ties were diligently pressed through a combination of silk and tissue paper. Salib and his co-workers were masters of a very ancient art.

Prince Rashid loved skiing, so we trekked to St. Moritz, Gstaad, Val d'Isere, Sun Valley, and Aspen. Wherever the snow was powdery, new, and in abundance, off we would go. Weather was never an impediment for anything we did. If we had a party in France and it was cloudy, he would fly everyone to Italy, where it was sunny. With such wealth why make do when perfection is just a private jet stop away? After several months, however, I began to realize why his aides only stayed for a short time. The pace was exhilarating but ultimately exhausting. In the ten months I had been traveling with the Prince no one ever took a day off. We rarely stayed in one city for more than a few days. The immense organization involved in packing, traveling, and relocating the Prince and his entourage was overwhelming.

I always kept up to $500,000 cash in the safe on the jet—"play money" as the Prince called it—and dealt only with the head of a major accounting firm in London who kept track of our worldwide expenses. He sent couriers from Switzerland to replenish our funds as required. My salary was deposited directly into my London bank each month, but with all my expenses paid and no free time to shop or socialize, I never touched it for the entire year.

There was a strong bond of friendship between Prince Rashid and myself. Unlike many cultures, Arabs value male bonding and are not inhibited about expressing affection between themselves. My year with the Prince offered a glimpse into a world only a very privileged few can ever afford—or indeed, have the imagination, energy, and adventurous spirit to create.

At the end of our year of living extravagantly, Prince Rashid had to return to his country. He asked me if I would continue to serve him but it required living half of the year in Saudia Arabia—an extremely rigid society compared to Europe and America. During our year together we shared a magical experience, but it was time to move on.

I kept in touch with Prince Rashid for many years, but we eventually drifted back into our diverse cultures. He is currently one of his country's great leaders.

As a bonus for my one year of devotion, he presented me with an exquisite five-carat ruby ring worth a small fortune. Sadly, it was stolen many years later from my London home. Although the ring is gone, the memories of a very special and unique experience remain.

Eight

After my year of endless travels with Prince Rashid I felt an extended vacation was definitely in order. A French nobleman and his wife, whom I had met at one of Lady Lavistock's parties, invited me to spend a month with them in Corfu. They had recently built an architecturally stunning villa on a hillside overlooking the Aegean Sea. I was certain the tranquil Greek waters would provide a welcome change from the bustling cities I had recently visited. For thirty-one uninterrupted days I did nothing but swim, snorkel, and sun myself under sultry Greek skies.

At the end of the holiday we decided to return to London via Cap d'Antibes. I booked a suite for the weekend at the Hotel du Cap, one of the most luxurious hotels in the world. Shortly after we arrived I telephoned M.S. to inquire about his health: He had recently undergone minor surgery. In his typically exuberant and generous style, he announced, "I'm recuperating by having a dinner party tonight! I insist you come and bring your friends."

I informed the Marquis and his wife of the invitation, which they were only too happy to accept. We dressed in our finest evening wear and drove along the winding seaside rode to M.S.'s villa. As I walked into the main salon I saw the elegant frame of a woman in a black taffeta gown silhouetted against a brilliant white piano. She was sipping champagne and swaying to the sounds of Cole Porter. The moment she turned her raven-haired head I recognized the unmistakably gentle eyes and inviting smile of La Contessa. I was captivated anew by her enchanting appearance. Although the world is filled with many lovely women, few possess an inner beauty transcending their physical appearance. Those who do are like poetry in motion. They rise above the mediocrity of everyday life and remind us why Adam so willingly sacrificed a rib. Such women inspire painters to create an eternal glimpse of the soul, and musicians to capture the everlasting cry of the heart. La Contessa was, indeed, such a woman.

It had been almost two years since our last meeting. I approached her and reintroduced myself. La Contessa assured me that I was not the type of person one easily forgot; she insisted I call her Sacha. We reminisced over a glass of Cristal about our days with M.S. in Monte Carlo. When dinner was announced I took her arm in mine and escorted her to the terrace of the main salon. Five tables of ten had meticulously been set with Limoges and Baccarat. I was pleased and surprised to find my place card next to Sacha's. (Years later M.S. confessed that he had telephoned Sacha after speaking with me. She had wanted to employ me ever since we met in 1976, but the timing wasn't right. They both hoped that M.S.'s

106

dinner party would provide the proper occasion to resolve that domestic dilemma.)

Between the vichysoisse and the blanquette de veau I entertained Sacha with the highlights of my adventures with the Prince.

"You should write a book about your extraordinary experiences," she suggested with a grin.

I told her I was looking for a new adventure—perhaps focus my energies on a romance instead of an employer. Financially I was in no hurry to return to work. I had not touched my salary or savings for the entire year. With no specific plans, I decided to wait and see what might unfold.

Sacha and I rather rudely ignored the other dinner guests, conversing non-stop until the floating islands arrived. I was impressed with the way she interacted with the waiters, always acknowledging their every effort with a "please" or "thank you." I learned that she owned homes in London, Paris, Ville France-sur-Mer, St. Moritz, Geneva, Bavaria, Italy, Greece, New York, and Aspen and had a newly acquired farm in Tuscany. Deciding to make it an even dozen, she was currently looking for something smart in Beverly Hills. I sensed a restless spirit and a serious shopper—two traits with which I could easily identify.

Unlike in most formal households, M.S. did not separate his guests after dinner. He believed men were often boring when isolated from their colorful counterparts. His progressive attitude allowed me the opportunity to talk further with Sacha. After coffee and liqueurs we walked to the garden to see the ocean view.

Under a magnitude of stars which sparkled as brightly as Sacha's eyes, I received my next job offer.

"Would you like to travel with me around the world and help organize my life? I know M.S. doesn't need your services. The majordomo I inherited twenty years ago from my mother is happy to retire and run my estate in Bavaria. He's tired of traveling. You are educated, charming, not intimidated by my life-style or afraid to spend the money required to maintain it. Come with me to visit my homes and make your decision after that period."

I was intrigued—not so much with the job but definitely with the lady. Sometimes you accept a position because of the work; other times because of who you'll be working with; I knew that if I accepted Sacha's offer it would be for the latter. I told her that I was flattered; I would think it over and telephone her in a few days with an answer.

Although I had traveled briefly with La Contessa when I was working for M.S., I knew very little about her background. During the drive back to the hotel, the Marquis' wife was only too eager to provide me with all of the details. La Contessa, like Prince Rashid, had lived a life of extreme indulgence. At sixteen she had a pet leopard which rode with her in a Mercedes 600 pullman limousine. She loved these particular automobiles and kept one parked in front of each home. Her favorite car, however, was the fast and sleek Aston Martin Lagonda. She owned several—all painted her favorite midnight blue.

La Contessa was twice married, twice divorced. Her first husband was compulsively possessive and jealous.

Husband number two, a poor Count who put on airs,

was a gigolo. Having acquired a wealthy wife, he proceeded to abuse his position through his extravagant and boorish behavior. He was both intimidated by and in love with La Contessa's wealth—an unpleasant combination which soon terminated marriage number two.

I was surprised to learn she had survived two unhappy marriages. La Contessa carried none of the emotional baggage usually associated with such unpleasant experiences.

By the time I returned to London I had made my decision: I accepted Sacha's offer to visit her many homes. She would certainly be a charming companion for a globe-trotting tour. I was also intrigued with the idea of exploring New York and Los Angeles for the first time. Having visited almost every other continent, I had yet to conquer America. After a brief telephone conversation, we agreed to meet the following week at her Eaton Square home to plan our strategy.

During our luncheon meeting the following Thursday we decided to begin our tour in Los Angeles and work our way East to Aspen, New York, and Europe.

"Plan to be away for three or four months," she stated quite matter of factly. "And there will be many social engagements en route," she added with a mischievous glint in her eye. "Whatever you need we'll purchase along the way."

At the conclusion of our tour I was to inform Sacha if I chose to accept the position on a full-time basis. She christened our trip "The Season of Adventure."

Sacha never mentioned money; she instructed me to telephone Herr Gunther in Geneva to discuss all of the financial arrangements. Because of her vast wealth she had separate offices tracking investments, holdings, and expenditures. Herr Gunther was the chief accountant in charge of expenditures. I chatted briefly with the very business-like German; we quickly arrived at an agreement. Herr Gunther informed me that La Contessa never handled cash—that would be my job. A few days before we left I received $100,000 for petty cash and several credit cards—those modern-day magic wands which transform desire into reality.

We began our tour aboard La Contessa's 747 jet. Her entourage consisted of: a secretary, a chef, a lady's maid, a hairdresser/beauty consultant, two pilots, three stewards, and two bodyguards. She frequently joked about the guards, stating, "They're not for me. They're for the jewels, dear!" referring to her $20 million collection which traveled with her everywhere.

I was extremely excited by the prospect of visiting Los Angeles for the first time. I couldn't wait to drive to Malibu to see if it resembled Pacific Plaza. Two days before our Season of Adventure began, I had attended a private party at the fashionable London club Annabel's. I had met a Beverly Hills entertainment lawyer who was in the midst of negotiating a multi-million-dollar contract for her star client. When I mentioned I would be visiting Los Angeles she offered some free advice.

"Look, honey," she began in an overly endearing tone. "To be successful in that town four things are essential: a good address; an expensive, sexy car; money; and knowing the art of bullshitting. Once you arrive in the land of silk and money you'll never want to leave. Beverly Hills is God's promised land. Forget dirty, dusty Israel.

BH is where a select group of people were meant to be."

Seventy-two hours after I received the unsolicited advice from the solicitor I stepped into the land of palm trees, mountains, and movies. I was fascinated by the city's picture-postcard perfection. Everyone seemed to be so polite with their "Have a nice day" and "How are you doing?" Everywhere I looked I saw smiling faces with movie-star teeth, and well-tanned bodies that rippled in the sun.

Sacha, myself, and two friends had luncheon at The Bistro Gardens—a watering hole for "the haves, almost haves and recently hads." The women were impeccably attired. I was surprised to see an elderly lady arrive in a *full sable*. Mind you, it was eighty degrees, but from the lack of reaction she received, everyone obviously considered her attire perfectly normal. I was also amazed at the amount of jewelry women wore during the day. I soon learned that in Beverly Hills, if you had it, you flaunted it.

Our entourage stayed at The Beverly Hills Hotel in an array of bungalows and suites. A variety of rental cars were at our disposal: a Rolls and a driver for Sacha; a Mercedes sedan for her secretary and lady's maid; a BMW for the chef; and a Mercedes 450SL for me. Sacha treated her staff exceptionally well and offered them every possible luxury.

We remained in Los Angeles much longer than originally planned: House-hunting proved to be a tedious and time-consuming experience. An elite group of real-estate agents cater to the stars and the super rich—individuals who think nothing of spending $5 million for a teardown or $3.5 million for a three-bedroom that "has enormous potential but needs work." The agents are

111

super-tanned, super-toned, and super-slick. After three weeks of looking at Neo-Tudor, Mock Tudor, Tudor, English Country Manor, French Château, Spanish Contemporary, and Contemporary, I finally saw a house worthy of its asking price: a contemporary Bel Air mansion with walls of glass offering a breathtaking view of the world. The main house was surrounded by manicured grounds, a swimming pool, tennis court, and an eight-car garage which I envisioned would soon be filled with German and Italian imports.

I drove Sacha to view the house. She detested being trapped and pushed into decisions by aggressive, sales-hungry real-estate agents. After a quick five-minute tour she said, "I'll take it." I notified Herr Gunther; a check for $5.8 million was Federal Expressed from Geneva the next day.

Time did not exist for Sacha; three days, three months, three years—it was all the same. She was not in a hurry to get anywhere because she had no commitments or specific plans. One weekend we flew to Aspen. I inspected her mountaintop home, beautifully furnished contemporary-style. We had dinner at Un Citi Banque and flew back to Los Angeles the next day.

As soon as a decorator had been hired for the new Bel Air home our entourage flew east to see how renovations on the Fifth Avenue apartment were progressing. It was my first visit to New York City. I felt like a five-year-old who was attending the circus for the first time. As we helicoptered into Manhattan from the airport I felt hypnotized by the rhythms of the city. Everywhere I looked there was a continual flow of people, automobiles, taxis, trucks—all moving with a "life or death" urgency to their various destinations. Tall buildings jutted out of the landscape like a warrior's dangerous spears. The arrogance of glass and steel skyscrapers towering over historical buildings seemed to suggest a culture which enthusiastically supported progress—at whatever cost. Horns honking, people pushing, sirens screaming: It was the most exciting city I had ever seen.

Admittedly, traveling in the company of a billionairess provides one with a unique perspective. Even though I had only been traveling with Sacha for nine weeks, I felt the position would suit me. I knew that the days ahead would be time-consuming and very demanding. But I was prepared.

We stayed at the Sherry Netherland with the usual arrangement of lavish suites. Our first morning we arose quite early to allow us a full day to tour the new apartment. I soon learned that despite the fact that New York is an extremely fast-paced city, there is nothing speedy about the process of renovating. We walked into an apartment which was supposed to have been near completion only to find half-built walls, wires hanging from the ceiling, plaster dust coating every visible surface, and several commodes in the foyer which had yet to find their appropriate resting place. I immediately organized a series of meetings with the contractors and decorators; they reassured us that all work would be completed in three months. Although we had every reason to doubt them, Sacha and I smiled, thanked them for their efforts, and decided to move on to Europe. The night before we left we dined at The River Café, a Brooklyn restaurant famous for its view of the Manhattan skyline. Little did I know then

that I would eventually make my permanent home somewhere below those beautifully twinkling lights.

We left the next morning for Athens; during the next
six-month period we worked our way through Rome,
Positano, Milan, Tuscany, Bavaria, Munich, Geneva,
Ville France-sur-Mer, St. Moritz, Paris, and our point of
origin—London. What was supposed to have been a
three-month tour had lasted nine months! During that
period I had visited magnificent homes and hotels, and
had met a variety of colorful and fascinating people.
Sacha and I became very good friends through our travels; although we cared for each other and often flirted, we
never crossed the fine line from a professional into a
personal relationship. We had a long discussion about
our Season of Adventure, during which I accepted the
position of majordomo. In retrospect, it was one of the
most happy and rewarding periods of my life. Of all my
employers, Sacha was by far the easiest to get along with.

My first assignment as Sacha's permanent majordomo
was to staff the newly decorated Bel Air mansion and
begin planning a spectacular party for her arrival. Her
secretary, Anita, gave me a guest list with one hundred
names—mostly Europeans. Of all the duties a majordomo may be required to perform, party planning definitely ranks in the top three. Because this was the first
celebration I had been assigned to organize for Sacha, I
threw all of my energy into planning something spectacular.

I created my version of "A Midsummer Night's
Dream." With the help of a set design company, an enormous white and green muslin tent was constructed

114

around the beautifully landscaped gardens. Green silk walls and moss-colored carpet helped transform the interior into a fairy grotto. Small twinkling lights hung from the ceiling in the shape of various constellations. The tables and chairs were draped in green and white silk which had been embroidered with faux pearls. A fish pond with a hidden Fiberglas platform would create the illusion that the orchestra was playing on water.

The wait staff dressed (or undressed, as the case may be) as pixies, fairies, nymphs, or elves to help complete the adult fairy-tale setting. Sacha looked stunning in a white silk and taffeta off-the-shoulder gown, the bodice embroidered with faux pearls. Her outfit was accessorized with a triple strand choker of diamonds and pearls with matching bracelet and earrings. It was an enchanting and extremely successful evening.

For the next six months I traveled around the world overseeing the domestic organization of the Contessa's kingdom. In total, I was responsible for twelve homes, one hundred staff members, and an annual budget of ten million dollars (excluding parties and any renovations or redecorating). I performed my job with the knowledge that I could make decisions without being second-guessed, which was very important to me. During a typical day, I might make a hundred different decisions—anything and everything from deciding on the particular glassware for a dinner party to the firing of a staff member. If I had to get approval, or if an employer was continually looking over my shoulder, it would be impossible to accomplish anything. La Contessa gave me free reign to perform my duties as I saw fit.

I appointed an executive housekeeper in each home who ran the staff on a day-to-day basis. My executive housekeepers and I were in constant communication. Every home was always ready. La Contessa had no schedule and what schedule there was could change at a moment's notice. Employees were paid above the going rate and I hired only the best people available. Each live-in staff member had his or her own luxuriously equipped private room, a new car, and generous time-off. At Christmas La Contessa handed out sizable bonuses and gave each of her employees a carefully selected gift.

On December 23, 1978, I flew to England to spend the holidays with my relatives. Because of the never-ending demands of my profession I had not seen my family for quite some time. Grandad had died earlier that year of a heart attack; my mother gave up her home to live with and care for my grandmother. Nansy was quite frail, devastated by the loss of her husband. She had never recovered from Roland's death. I now feared her health and spirit would continue in a downward spiral. Although I didn't know it at the time, it would be the last Christmas I would spend with them for many years.

In early January, I flew to Aspen, where La Contessa was pursuing a new love interest. She had all of her potential suitors investigated by an ex-Interpol agent who worked as a private detective. A particularly dashing fifty-year-old Arabian Prince who appeared to have almost as much money as La Contessa passed all the necessary tests. Sacha juggled him with a thirty-year-old Brazilian boy. He was extraordinarily handsome and from an affluent

South American family, but far too immature to be anything more than a pretty diversion.

During the next several months we were busy preparing for the arrival of La Contessa's sleek new toy, a 180-foot Italian yacht, *Alexandria,* which Sacha had named for her mother. We planned to sail through the Greek islands, around the Mediterranean, and helicopter periodically to her various homes. We also began making arrangements for a grand expedition to the Far East, which we had been talking about for almost a year.

Summer arrived and so did The Butterfly Ball, Ascot and The Queen's Garden Party—all major events in the English social calendar. Sacha had been the wife of an Earl. She had many titled friends in the British aristocracy and always received an invitation to the Royal Enclosure. This particular year M.S. gave a grand Ascot party at his country home. During the festivities Sacha fell in love with a married man of royal blood. Although this particular Duke was financially needy, with large estates to maintain and an extravagant and ill-tempered wife, Sacha remained quite passionate about him. She now had three men to juggle—not all that difficult if you have multiple homes.

The Butterfly Ball is held in Berkley Square, which is closed off for the evening. The gala is frequented by all the young and old members of the aristocracy. Sacha gave a dinner at that fashionable club Annabel's, just across the street from the ball. Her beau of the evening was the young Brazilian stud. I watched closely when the new Duke in Sacha's life arrived accompanied by his stern wife. The Duchess had a face that could crack ice. No wonder he wanted to upgrade to the beautiful Contessa.

117

Midway through the evening Sacha managed to slip away with the Duke—unnoticed by everyone except for myself, who had eyes and ears everywhere. They reappeared separately a few hours later. During her husband's absence the Duchess met someone at the ball who melted her sour face. Two months later she decided to terminate her marriage, leaving the Duke free to pursue a relationship with his Italian Contessa. Sacha alternated her affections for many months between the Duke, the Arabian Prince and the young Brazilian boy-toy. As she continued her search for true love I continued traveling between her homes and the yacht.

During my third year with La Contessa, we finally went on our cruise to the Far East: Singapore, Thailand, India, Ceylon, Bali, and Australia. I left Sacha in Ceylon and flew back to Los Angeles to organize a party which was canceled at the last minute. In Bali, Sacha met a wealthy Australian publisher. She spent the next three months between the Far East and Australia and then took a three-month cruise throughout the Pacific Ocean via Fiji, Cook Islands, Tahiti, and Hawaii. Six months after I had left her in Ceylon, she finally returned to Beverly Hills. It was unlike her to spend so much time with a single companion; I felt this was the real thing for her. The Australian was witty, charming, widowed, very rich, and surprisingly short.

As soon as Sacha arrived at her Bel Air home, she quickly filled me in on her latest romance. She told me her Aussie gent was planning to retire; they were going to marry soon and travel for a year. She could never live in Australia and he did not like America so they planned to build a large residence in Marbella, where they would live semi-permanently. Marbella has a lovely climate and is very sophisticated and beautiful. She had decided to sell all of her American residences. Only her homes in London and Europe would remain.

Sacha knew how fond I had grown of America and that I might not be happy spending the majority of my time in Marbella. She asked if I would at least help with the transition.

Although I had fallen in love with America and decided to live in Los Angeles, I agreed to stay for six months to settle them into their new life together. I still preferred working for single people, favoring one direct link to authority; once again I would leave a position due to someone's marriage.

The homes were sold; I helped pack and ship all the contents to Europe. Sacha had a quiet Swiss wedding and lived happily ever after. She and her husband spend time traveling or relaxing at their magical villa in Marbella.

I loved every moment of the years I spent with La Contessa, who to this day still keeps her title and maiden name. She is truly a lady in every respect, and I have always had an open invitation to pick up where I left off at any time.

Nine

During my association with La Contessa I made numerous social and professional contacts. In Los Angeles—a city where "who you *know*" takes precedence over "who you *are*"—contacts are like pieces of a very elaborate puzzle. The trick is in finding those *particular* pieces which will help you complete the puzzle as quickly as possible. If you want to be a successful screenwriter and you are fortunate enough to know Michael Ovitz (head of the powerful Creative Arts Agency) chances are you will complete your puzzle in three minutes or less. If, however, your most important contact is a twenty-two-year old Harvard graduate working in the mail room of The William Morris Agency, you may not see the full picture for several years. The pace at which you progress is contingent upon finding the "key" pieces.

I was fortunate to have found several key pieces through my affiliation with La Contessa. She led me to certain individuals who helped speed the assembly of a particular picture I was trying to create: a stimulating and financially rewarding life for myself in America. In 1980, I began assembling my puzzle with three exceptionally diverse personalities: an unhappy heiress to a family fortune; a Beverly Hills housewife who wanted to upgrade her image; and a wild and unruly rock star who had a proclivity for group sex.

Shortly after I left La Contessa's employ I rented a contemporary two-bedroom house on Palm Drive. In a black Mercedes 450SL I navigated Los Angeles' maze of freeways, visiting friends from the beaches of Malibu to the winding roads of Beverly Hills. On an exceptionally hot August day I attended one of those barbecues for which Americans are famous. Over a buffet of hamburgers, hotdogs, potato salad, and cole slaw, I met Elli Mayer Bryden, the Oscar Mayer heiress. We chatted briefly about various "puzzle pieces" we had in common. When she learned I was a majordomo she asked if I would be interested in a temporary position. Elli was planning to marry and relocate to Palm Beach; she needed assistance with the upcoming move. In retrospect, it seems as if my entire life has been devoted to people who are in a constant state of transition. I have seen more boxes than a UPS warehouse.

Although there was nothing exceptionally interesting about Elli's job offer, I found myself drawn in by her vulnerability. She had a glazed and far-away look in her eyes. Although I didn't know it at the time, Elli had seen more than her share of unhappiness. She reminded me of a frightened little girl who had lost her way home but was unable to ask for help. I think most of her adult life she had been trying to find her way back; I don't know if she

122

was ever successful. More than any of my previous employers, I felt that Elli needed my help; if I could ease her transition into a new beginning, the job would prove satisfying.

Elli had been married eight times to one unfortunate character after another—most apparently after her money. From what I gathered, the soon-to-be Husband No. 9 was no different than his predecessors: he had demanded a Rolls-Royce Corniche as proper enticement to walk down the aisle leading to matrimonial bliss.

Elli's greatest problem (other then her bad judgment in men) was a predilection for alcohol: She loved rum toddies for breakfast, Bloody Marys for lunch, and martinis for dinner—not the healthiest of diets for an anorexically inclined woman in her fifties. Although she should have been living the glamorous and carefree life of an heiress, her experiences had been far from happy. In addition to a string of bad marriages, two of her four children had committed suicide in their late teens. It was sad to see someone with so much who had so little personal satisfaction.

Through the real-estate agents I had met while househunting for La Contessa, I helped Elli sell her Trousdale estate. She temporarily relocated to The Beverly Hills Hotel until the paperwork was completed for her new Palm Beach villa. The deal, unfortunately, fell through at the last minute. Elli was stranded and in a panic. At her request, I rented a 6,600 square-foot beach house in Malibu and a penthouse condominium within walking distance of Rodeo Drive. The Malibu estate was quite magnificent: two acres of landscaped grounds with fountains, fruit orchard, tennis court and swimming pool. The main house featured a dining-room with hand-painted frescoes, sunken living room, and floor-to-ceiling windows providing stunning ocean views. The platinum blonde real-estate agent assured me that because I was a favored client she would get me a "deal": $3.8 million to purchase or $22,000 a month to rent.

While I organized the two new residences, Elli forged ahead with her plans to marry. Three months after her wedding date the marriage was annulled. The Rolls-Royce, however, was not.

The unhappy heiress filled her days shopping, attending luncheon parties, and playing bridge with gal-pals like Gregory Peck's charming first wife Greta, and other wealthy single, widowed, or multi-divorced ladies.

During my early weeks with Elli I became increasingly alarmed by her alcohol consumption. The first time I saw her collapse at the dinner table I thought she had suffered a heart attack. One minute she had been laughing hysterically, the next she was face down in the consommé Mailène. I rushed to the phone and dialed 911. Marthe, her hefty German housekeeper, told me to sit down and finish my dinner.

"My mistress is merely drunk," she stated. "She has passed out. Again."

I was shocked to learn this might become part of some strange mealtime routine. The strong-armed Marthe lifted her pitiable employer and carried her to bed.

I was speechless. I had been exposed to people all my life who utilized drugs and alcohol to either enhance or diminish everyday realities. Never before had I witnessed someone who was so tortured that he or she was reduced to passing out at the dinner table. Many years later, when

124

I viewed the film *Reversal of Fortune,* I saw similarities between the lives of Sunny Von Bulow and Elli Mayer Bryden. I realized that women of great fortune are not always so fortunate.

Until I took control, Elli's judgment in hiring help was as misguided as her choice in men. When I began to interview potential chefs, Elli told me that (with the exception of Marthe) she had never been lucky with her household staff; one of her previous employees had even tried to murder her. Several years back, Elli had hired a large-framed Eastern European cook. She prepared some foreign concoction which Elli promptly sent back to the kitchen. The chef, however, was extremely sensitive about her cooking: she bolted into the dining room with a large butcher's knife and tried to silence her critical employer. Elli managed to lock herself in a bedroom and telephone the police before she became the main ingredient in a rare Hungarian stew. She later found out that the crazed cook had escaped from a sanatorium.

Despite her many problems, Elli could often be quite amusing. One day she waltzed me into the kitchen, opened the refrigerator, and removed a package of Oscar Mayer bacon. I wasn't familiar with American brands at the time; although I planned menus and occasionally prepared shopping lists, I rarely went to the supermarket. Elli tapped her index finger against the cellophane package and whispered, "This is my family. But don't tell anyone."

I was confused; I thought she was trying to tell me she hated her relatives and likened them to pigs. Marthe, who had witnessed our little scene and was laughing in

125

the background, later explained the significance of the "Mayer" name.

Elli, like many affluent people, did not wish to be thought of as rich. She frequently pleaded poverty, announcing that she was down to her last million. Like many heiresses, Elli lived in fear that someone would take advantage of her—which frequently happened. But when she wanted to assert herself, she trotted out the family name.

One morning we were having breakfast, reviewing the arrangements for her upcoming move. Marthe was on the telephone trying to sort out a grocery bill; she had apparently been charged for several deliveries she never received. Elli overheard the discussion and snatched the phone from Marthe's hands.

"Do you know who I am!?!" she asked in a very grandiose voice. "I am Elli *Mayer,* the *Oscar Mayer* heiress! If you don't give me proper satisfaction I'll remove my lunch meat from your store!"

Marthe and I tried to withhold our laughter as we listened to our semi-reclusive employer sort out her grocery bill.

I stayed with Elli for approximately four months, until she finally moved to Palm Beach. It was, overall, a depressing experience. Sadly, she died two years later of lung cancer.

My grandmother used to say, "Manners maketh man." I certainly found this to be true during my days in Los Angeles: I encountered many wealthy people who didn't have a clue as to how to behave properly or what to do with their newly acquired fortunes.

Many Beverly Hills residents are true Beverly Hill-billies—new-monied types who suddenly move from $50,000 houses to $5 million palaces. These people want to upgrade their life-style, but don't know how or where to go to get the necessary information. There is no School for the Recently Rich which teaches the difference between a $50 set of bed linens from J.C. Penney and a $5,000 set from Porthault or Pratesi. Many women who are used to spending $100 for a party dress are intimidated by the thought of buying a $10,000 Chanel suit—even if their husbands encourage them to do so. They need someone to help recreate and define a new affluent life-style. I had the pleasure to transform the lives of one such couple.

Harry and Barbara made millions (almost) overnight. Harry was a business manager who finally landed a cash cow of a client—someone who unexpectedly became one of the highest paid individuals in the entertainment industry. As soon as his 10 percent began rolling in, he rented a palatial Beverly Hills estate. The couple planned to find a large piece of land and eventually build their dream house.

Barbara was Harry's former secretary, who had apparently taken more than her fair share of dictation: At nineteen she was impregnated by her forty-one-year-old employer. Harry's wife promptly exchanged her husband for her husband's money. Harry then married Barbara and they struggled along for several years. By the time I met Barbara, however, she was twenty-five, the mother of three, and manageress of a large estate with a staff of ten.

I was introduced to the Beverly Hills housewife by Allison, a rather small "puzzle piece" from my days in London. Allison telephoned and asked if I would be willing to help an upwardly mobile young woman whose education in social graces was non-existent—she had become somewhat of an embarrassment to her socially inclined husband. My interest was titilated; I was between jobs and could sense a challenge when it was presented. I agreed to meet with the potential pupil the following day.

I dressed in a navy summer suit with my signature bow tie—the epitome of British formality. As I drove past an iron gate with the initial "S" blazoned in bright gold, I wondered if my English acquaintance had overstated her friend's dilemma. The moment I pressed the doorbell and heard a voice which could shatter glass, I knew Allison had been kind.

"I'll get it, guyz!" a high-pitched voice shrieked.

I next heard what sounded like the flip-flapping of beach sandals against a marble floor. Suddenly it stopped; the door flew open. As I stared at the figure before me my lips parted ever so slightly in amazement. A small-framed woman in a loud print jogging suit was frantically chewing gum. Atop her head sat a crown of hot-pink curlers. I glimpsed a white-jacketed butler in the background who looked helpless and confused. With such a badly dressed and ill-mannered housekeeper, I could immediately see why it was a poorly run establishment.

I introduced myself and informed the gum-chewing creature that I had an appointment with the lady of the house.

"There's no ladies here," she replied with the wink of a heavily mascaraed eye. "But comeoninanyway. I'm Barbara. Pleasetomeetya."

128

I thought about rushing back to my car to retrieve a foreign language dictionary, but I wasn't sure *what* foreign language this energetic young woman was uttering.

Barbara slammed the door and led the way to the library, jabbering non-stop; I desperately searched the walls of the hallway for some type of volume control. We sat opposite each other in the darkly paneled library and she offered me a drink. I opted for a chilled Pelegrino. She asked for her "usual," which aroused my curiosity. Five minutes later the butler returned with a tray bearing my water and a Coke. Barbara happily swigged from the can and proceeded to tell me her story, repeating much of what I had already learned from Allison. Although she was completely lacking in social graces, I could see she had an engaging personality and enormous potential.

"I wanna learn how to talk nice, ya know? Entertain, run a house, dress smart, shop smart, eat like a lady, yaknowwhadImean?

I assured her I understood what the problem was.

"C'mon now. Lemee show ya the house." Shortly after we began our tour the door bell rang. Like a Pavlovian dog, she dashed to the foyer, almost knocking over the butler in the process. He looked at me and rolled his eyes. Barbara certainly found the prospect of visitors exciting.

"It was just a Fed-Ex for my hubby." She escorted me upstairs to the master suite and showed me walk-in closets stuffed with expensive but unsuitable clothing. The style, fabrics, and colors were reminiscent of a Las Vegas showgirl's.

While I was inspecting her wardrobe Barbara glanced out the window and suddenly screamed, "OHMY-GOD!!!"

I ran for cover, thinking we were about to become the victims of some crazed Beverly Hills sniper.

"I forgot I've got to pick up the kids," she announced as she began to run out the door. "They're at the movies. Come on. We'll talk more in the car."

I caught my breath and followed her to the double doors of a cavernous garage. She pressed a switch, revealing "his and her" white Corniche convertibles, a Ferrari, and a Mercedes 450SL. Apparently her husband's client was making as much money as all of the tabloids had reported. Barbara jumped into the nearest Corniche (still modeling her hot-pink crown) and we sped down the driveway. I pulled out my black Ray Bans and devised a plan in case I was recognized: I would tell anyone who asked that I had been kidnapped by a woman who had become obsessed with the film *Diary of a Mad Housewife*.

We picked up her three unruly children from a nearby cinema and then made a last-minute stop at the market. By the time we returned I realized my work was cut out for me. Despite her many faults, I admired Barbara's forthright approach to learning. There is something endearing about anyone who is willing to admit ignorance in a particular area and then make an effort to improve. Barbara's enthusiasm was quite infectious; I told her I would accept the assignment.

My new pupil began jumping up and down with excitement. You would have thought she had just been appointed head cheerleader for the football team.

"Can we start tomorrow?" she asked. "Please, please! I don't want to waste another day."

I told her tomorrow would be fine.

"By the way, how much doyawant?" she asked, opening a Gucci bag stuffed with $100 bills.

I smiled and briefly thought of my previous employers, who never even mentioned money. After learning my hourly fee she shoved a wad of bills into my hand.

"There's five thou'. Lemme know when it's used up. See ya tomorrow, hon. I can't wait!"

As I drove down the driveway past the golden S, I thought I glimpsed a very excitable young lady in my rearview mirror turning cartwheels on the lawn.

When I met with Barbara the next day I told her that if I was going to help transform her into the person she wished to become I would have to be forthright.

"Look hon," she said, "you can tell me anything you want. That's what I'm payin' ya for."

I suggested that before we begin her instruction we visit a friend of mine who would provide her with the best possible example of how a proper lady should behave. I wanted Barbara to have some frame of reference for certain topics I would be addressing. I had arranged for us to take afternoon tea with Lady Beatrice, a lovely woman whom I had know for many years in England. Lady Beatrice had recently relocated to Los Angeles to be near her three grandchildren.

Barbara loved the idea of visiting "royalty"; she quickly ran upstairs to change. Thirty minutes later she came down in some purple fringed atrocity. I politely gave her the first of what would be a long list of rules.

"One never, *ever* wears fringe of any kind—not to a rodeo, not to a square dance, not *ever*."

I accompanied her upstairs and selected the least of-

131

fensive item I could find: a Laura Ashley print dress accessorized with pearl earrings.

We drove to Lady Beatrice's Pasadena residence and rang the bell. Henley, the butler, greeted us.

"Good afternoon," he offered with a slight nod of the head. "Madam is expecting you both. Follow me, please."

Lady Beatrice greeted us in a dark Chanel suit with a single strand of pearls draped around her neck.

"Desmond, my dear. How have you been? I haven't had the pleasure of your company since M.S.'s last party at Ascot."

I made all of the necessary introductions. Once we were seated in the rose-colored drawing room Henley poured tea from a three-hundred-year-old silver tea service. Barbara was absolutely beside herself with excitement; she followed my instruction to observe and not ask too many questions. She watched carefully as Lady Beatrice took small sips of tea from a porcelain cup and the most infinitesimal bites of a digestive biscuit.

"I must say, I'm quite impressed with your initiative, young lady," Lady Beatrice declared. "A willingness to improve oneself at any age is admirable."

Lady Beatrice explained that she was disappointed by the lack of proper social breeding amongst many of Los Angeles' more affluent women. She'd recently given a charity fund-raising tea party and invited some nouveau riche Beverly Hills wives—many of whom arrived terribly overdressed.

"It was a tea party, mind you, not some grand ball. One of the young wives wore an extremely short cocktail dress with fringe around the hem! Can you imagine!"

132

Barbara and I exchanged a quick smile while Lady Beatrice continued with her description of the party.

"Another woman arrived forty minutes late wearing a silver beaded jacket with matching hat and shoes. She was lit up like a Christmas tree with her overabundance of jewelry! A proper lady should always dress simply for tea and not be overly accessorized. I want you to take note, my dear, just because one *has* it all doesn't mean to say one has to *wear* it all on a single occasion."

As I had hoped, Lady Beatrice was in the midst of one of her diatribes on social etiquette. Barbara listened attentively and nodded in agreement.

Lady Beatrice next remarked on a recent picture she had seen of one of New York City's leading socialites in a strapless evening dress.

"My dears, can you imagine anything so vulgar! No lady of any respectability—unless she is *exceedingly* well toned—would dream of wearing a dress which displays one's flesh sagging off the bones!"

I told the women about the time my mother had briefly visited me in New York. She had seen a picture of the same creature Lady Beatrice was describing and had asked why a female impersonator was being featured in a woman's fashion magazine. I informed my mother that the female in question was no drag queen—she was one of New York's leading new socialites.

To which my mother had replied, "They're so hard and brash. Where do they come from?"

After an hour had passed I thanked Lady Beatrice for tea; she wished us the best of luck in our endeavor.

* * *

During our drive back from Pasadena, Barbara chattered endlessly. She was a very eager and attentive pupil. I felt certain that with enough time and guidance she would transform herself into an elegant social butterfly.

When we returned I gave my anxious student ten tips for becoming a lady:

> First: The gum has to go! Ladies do not chew gum. Ever.
>
> Second: Wearing rollers around the house all day—let alone the neighborhood—is forbidden. You live in Beverly Hills, a neighborhood where even the wrong color car can cause a scandal. I'll hire a hairdresser to come to the house. The bleached blonde look has got to go. I know a makeup artist who can properly instruct you. The supply of press-on nails and pink lip gloss can be thrown away.
>
> Three: Clothes will be selected for style, color, and their ability to enhance your particular physique.
>
> Four: Never answer the door. That is why you have hired a butler. It only confuses and embarrasses the poor man when you try to race him to the doorknob.
>
> Five: A lady does not rush in and out of her kitchen. You have a chef with whom you will meet once a day to review menus. Trust her to do the work without your constant supervision.
>
> Six: Your children are a reflection of you. We must hire a strict governess to control and educate them just as I am trying to educate you. Discipline at an early age is vital.

Seven: It is not necessary for you to grocery shop. Let your staff do that for you.

Eight: I will hire a personal trainer to work with you three times a week. In order to walk and carry yourself like a lady you will need to be in proper shape.

Nine: Never, never, never drink out of a can. It is extremely unlady-like and most unhygenic. By the look of the cabinets you must have sixty thousand dollars' worth of crystal. Use it.

Ten: A lady speaks proper English and uses complete sentences. I will work with you personally in this particular area.

Barbara was slightly overwhelmed. She laughed and said, "I'll be like Eliza Doolittle in *My Fair Lady,* won't I?"

I thought of Audrey Hepburn and hoped for the best.

The undertaking was enormous but the rewards were great. Within three months I had reorganized her house, trained the staff, hired a proper British governess, and transformed a frenetic and fast-talking girl into an elegant and sophisticated young lady. We purchased an entirely new wardrobe, experimented with hair and makeup, and ate at the most exclusive restaurants, where I taught proper table etiquette and menu and wine selection. Expressions such as "Yeah sure" and "Okay" were replaced by "Of course" and "Certainly." Contractions like "Hihowyadoin' " and "Dijaseeumanywhere?" became as extinct as snack trays in front of the large-screen television. Harry (whom I didn't meet for weeks) eventually joined us for formal dinners. He was a handsome and charming gentleman thrilled with his wife's progress.

During the fourth month of our training I decided it was time to put Barbara to the test: I instructed her to organize a formal dinner party for twelve. She was responsible for making all the decisions, from menu selection to table arrangements and wardrobe. I don't think most people (unless they have done it themselves) can appreciate the amount of work involved in organizing an elegant dinner party. As an added incentive I invited Lady Beatrice.

The day of her "final exam" Barbara was understandably nervous. I tried to stay in the background so she wouldn't feel as if her every move was being scrutinized. Although she panicked twice and braced herself with a few glasses of champagne before the guests arrived, Barbara had no need to worry: The dinner party was a tremendous success. I was proud of my student and, more important, she was proud of her own achievement. The next day Barbara received the best possible report card: a phalaenopsis orchid with a note attached that read, "Congratulations, young lady, on a job well done!—Lady Beatrice."

The total cost of transforming Barbara was enormous; we later joked about her "million-dollar make-over." But vast wealth is not a prerequisite for self-improvement of any kind. I have met secretaries earning less than $25,000 a year who are well-mannered, beautifully attired, and elegant examples of what it means to be a lady. The most important requirement in any kind of transformation is a strong desire to better oneself. Money is merely one of several tools toward achieving that end—

but it is not the only one. Industry and initiative will often produce more concrete results than the greatest fortune.

Barbara was an admirable pupil who learned her lessons well. She is currently one of Beverly Hills' leading hostesses. She eventually built her dream house and is still happily married to Harry—a remarkable achievement considering Hollywood's divorce rate. I eventually introduced her to many of my aristocratic friends in England. Each year she sits in The Royal Enclosure, sipping champagne and eating strawberries.

Eliza Doolittle returned to Ascot once again.

I next accepted a brief assignment with a six-foot-two-inch muscular rock star whose new-found fame had afforded him a luxurious life-style. The young man with long blond hair needed someone to organize and furnish a recently purchased Malibu beach house, hire and train a staff, and arrange a few parties. It seemed simple enough compared to jobs I had held in the past. Little did I know that when one enters the crazy, chaotic world of rock 'n' roll, it's like a visit to a very strange planet.

My rock star was guilty of the "bad-boy" syndrome: wild, wanton, ill-mannered and ill-kempt, but all done with a boyish humor which made it slightly more tolerable. To say he lived like a pig would be a disservice to barnyard creatures everywhere. He preferred roaming the house wearing nothing but a smile, which offended most of the female staff members. Those who were not offended were frequently "distracted" from their work. It was not surprising that I went through help as quickly as he went through drugs.

His substance abuse and penchant for casual relationships became quite unnerving at times. It was not unusual to be awakened at 3 A.M. by the sound of blaring rock music, the smell of burning marijuana, and the sight of several unsavory characters engaging in sexual practices which might challenge the most experienced trollop. I am certainly no prude and have nothing against anyone's sexual preference, but even self-destruction and depravity can be done with a bit of style.

The few parties I organized were a waste of time. The only party supplies his guests required were sugarbowls full of cocaine and fishbowls full of marijuana cigarettes. I never saw whoever supplied these party favors; they "mysteriously" appeared. The rock star did pay well and was never rude to me personally. Although we were almost the same age, I made it quite clear that I wouldn't take any nonsense from him. It was a case of easy come, easy go; everything in every possible size and shape came and went through his doors.

A friend once lent him a house in Aspen for a week. He asked me to accompany him with a few butlers. (It was pointless trying to hire maids anymore.) The week was relatively peaceful by the rock star's standards. The final night, however, he entertained a most uninhibited group of individuals. After a few bottles of champagne everyone stripped off their clothes and jumped into the Jacuzzi (I am always amazed at how Americans love to socialize in hot water). I concluded that my services would not be required for quite some time and retreated to the privacy of the kitchen. Thirty minutes later someone buzzed me on the intercom and requested several more bottles of champagne. When I appeared, I couldn't quite distinguish the thirsty individual: Everyone was otherwise en-

138

gaged. I mustered as much of my British poise as I could and poured Moët into any empty glasses I could find, trying to avoid elbows and other protruding appendages.

When we returned to Los Angeles I decided to find a new position as soon as possible. Within two weeks I received a job offer. My association with the bad boy of rock led me to my next employer—one of the biggest puzzle pieces in the history of disco.

Ten

At 1:33 A.M. on a Wednesday morning I stood crouched over a stainless-steel sink, frantically trying to clean fish eggs off a cream suede loafer. My rock star was in the midst of a post-concert party at his newly furnished Malibu beach house. I had been serving caviar to a large-framed, inebriated woman who suddenly decided to perform her imitation of an octopus in heat. The spur-of-the-moment impression sent several spoonfuls of Beluga flying into the air and onto my new Italian shoes. I thrust the silver serving tray into a flailing tentacle and dashed into the kitchen to repair the damage. As I watched two hundred dollars' worth of black gold disappear down the drain I began listening to the voices in the next room. There is a distinctly unique rhythm to Hollywood parties—a three-step process which enables one to make contact with everyone present in twenty-two minutes or less.

Step 1: *The Kiss.*

Quickly kiss each cheek of the person you are greeting,

but never permit your lips to touch the naked flesh of another.

Step 2: *The Comment.*

Stretch your mouth into a twelve-inch smile (hopefully revealing thirty thousand dollars' worth of perfect teeth) and make a clever or complimentary remark.

Step 3: *The Laugh.*

Finally, with an "I'm clever—you're clever—we're all clever or we wouldn't be at this party" toss of the head, chuckle and move on to the next person. Repeat the process until you have endeared yourself to everyone in the room at least once.

Kiss, kiss. Comment. Laugh and move on. Kiss, kiss. Comment. Laugh and move on. The relentless rhythm of Hollywood at work.

While drying my shoe I listened to a woman who owned 15 percent of Hollywood's hottest actors expertly executing this technique.

Kiss, kiss.

"Sheila, you look so 'Edie Williams' in that purple plastic pantsuit. Call my secretary and we'll do Fiorucci's."

Kiss, kiss.

"Michael darling, I heard your album just went platinum. How delicious! Royalty heaven! Let's have lunch soon to count the pennies."

Kiss, kiss.

"Billy, closer dear, I have to whisper in your ear. I just scored some 'high C' which will have you singing arias for days. Meet me in the black marble bathroom in ten."

There was so much air-kissing going on in the next room it sounded like the final game of a championship

Ping-Pong tournament. The crowd was the usual mix of business suits, black leather, and a little Betsey Johnson thrown in for color. I slipped on the loafer, trying to decide if it was ruined. A handsomely dressed gentleman wandered into the kitchen and asked if he could get an espresso. Although I found the request somewhat unusual, his prevailing good manners persuaded me to deliver him unto the caffeinated gods.

We chatted briefly about my experiences working in Europe while I prepared the coffee. He seemed to be rather shy compared to the extroverted types in the next room performing an assortment of fish imitations. After a few minutes the coffee was ready. In addition to his thanks, the stylish gentleman offered his business card—a favorite Los Angeles pastime. He mentioned that he could use an assistant; if I was interested in moving from rock 'n' roll into disco I should give him a call. I thanked him for the compliment and he wandered back to the Ping-Pong match.

I glanced at the name on the card—"Giorgio Moroder"—but had no idea who he was. Someone mentioned Donna Summer, the disco diva whose long legs and even longer hair helped her writhe her way to the top of the charts. Giorgio was her producer and, until Donna "moaned" her way onto the scene with "Love to Love You Baby," most of his success had been in Europe. I was immediately attracted to his low-key, European style—a vast improvement over my bad boy of rock. I telephoned Giorgio the following week and was hired three days later.

*   *   *

I became Giorgio's right-hand man: butler, valet, cook, majordomo, travel agent, Mr. Fix-it—whatever he needed, I was ready to do.

Giorgio's glass-and-marble home was perched on a cliff in the exclusive Trousdale Estates section of Beverly Hills. Dubbed "The Ice Palace" because of its stark and severe decor, the architecturally stunning residence offered magnificent views in all directions. The Ice Palace featured a river of grey marble floors which flowed down to the pool area and beyond. Lalique-etched tables and contemporary Italian furniture instantly commanded one's attention in an otherwise vacant room. With the touch of a button, a studio-quality sound system pumped the latest music throughout the house; state-of-the-art televisions and video recorders suddenly appeared behind grey lacquer panels. The completely mirrored kitchen was as technologically sophisticated as the rest of the house, with every labor-saving device imaginable. In the garage, a black Rolls-Royce convertible and a bright red Ferrari completed the picture of Giorgio's success. D&D (Disco & Donna) had obviously been an extremely lucrative combination.

My first day on the job Giorgio asked me to retrieve a tape from his home and deliver it to the studio where he was working late into the night. A relatively simple request—or so I thought at the time. When I arrived and opened the front door I was startled by the sound of someone playing Chopin on the white grand piano. I frantically grabbed a glass ashtray and crept into the dimly lit living-room. I was shocked to find an elderly woman sitting on the piano stool, hunched over the keyboard. The music abruptly stopped.

144

"Who are you," I shouted from across the room. "What are you doing here?!"

The menacing creature did not respond to my query. I began to panic. Did the phantom piano player have a heart attack in the middle of her scherzo? Was this some bizarre new technique which burglars utilized if the owner unexpectedly arrived?

I cautiously approached the figure and was embarrassed to discover the musical mugger was actually a life-size mannequin. "Agatha" was one of Giorgio's more amusing state-of-the-art devices: a life-size, full-figured, piano-playing doorbell. Anytime someone opened the front door, Agatha enthusiastically began pounding the keys. She certainly was the life of all our parties.

On a typical day I arrived at the Ice Palace by 9 A.M. My first task was to remove my shoes: Giorgio's penchant for sleeping late and the grey marble floors throughout the house were not entirely compatible. People who work in the recording industry keep very unconventional hours, frequently working until dawn. I tip-toed around the house, setting up the pool area with several multi-lined telephones—Giorgio's lifeline to the world. At noon, I would serve brunch by the pool—usually fruit, ham, Beluga, and strong espresso coffee.

As morning stretched into afternoon an assortment of industry people began to arrive: secretaries, publicists, composers, film developers, agents, managers, and various key members of Giorgio Moroder Enterprises. In typical L.A. style, everyone dressed in sports shirts and short pants. They worked by the pool, making decisions that would expand Giorgio's financial empire. Projects at the

145

time ranged from a musical on Marilyn Monroe to a Kristy McNichol movie. In what I soon learned was typical Hollywood fashion, most of these ideas never got out of the development stage.

Giorgio loved a party, even if he was a little shy at the onset. Like many people I have worked for, he preferred to remain out of sight until everyone arrived. For most of our celebrations we opened the fully retractable floor-to-ceiling windows, which allowed the living-room to flow directly into the pool area, creating an enormous open-air entertainment space. Whenever I pressed the button and watched the wall of glass disappear, I felt that excitement and anticipation one feels at the rise of a Broadway curtain. It was definitely "showtime."

Giorgio's parties were lavishly catered events with very L.A.–styled food: mountains of fresh fruit, shrimp, lobster, a variety of salads, grilled chicken in lemon sauce—all kept in silver chaffing dishes and served by waiters who were as glamorous as the guests.

One evening, Giorgio gave a party for his brother Uli, an aspiring artist at the time. Because Giorgio preferred to remain out of sight until the party was in full swing, he designated me as "the official greeter." I stood by the front entrance in my dinner jacket and welcomed each individual, escorting any unaccompanied ladies into the gathering. In England and Europe it is considered improper for unescorted women to walk into a formal gathering alone. Of course, in Beverly Hills such rules were nonexistent. People came and went by themselves, in groups, with each others' spouses or with animals—no one seemed to notice. But Giorgio adhered to certain

European standards of entertaining which I could appreciate.

That evening, Lady Rothmere, the wife of a British newspaper tycoon, arrived unescorted. She was a buxom, high-spirited, English eccentric whose husband owned Harmsworth Press. I accompanied her into the living-room and introduced her to a fellow Englishwoman who worked in publishing.

Kiss, kiss.

"Call me Bubbles. I understand you're in the papers, darling. Perhaps you work for me. I own most of them, you know." She threw back her head and giggled. "You'll have to excuse me but I must push on."

Lady Rothmere had obviously perfected the three-step process.

Although she had only just arrived, Lady Rothmere suddenly decided to leave. She complimented me on *my* beautiful home, handed the waiter her glass, and swept out to a waiting limousine. I really think she had no idea whose party she was attending. First-timers frequently mistook me for Giorgio: I greeted guests, circulated freely, and made certain everyone had whatever they might need. Giorgio always kept a low profile. If you went by appearance alone, it was quite easy to mistake me for the disco genius.

Giorgio traveled frequently to Europe. His main recording studio, "Musicland Studios," was located in Munich. My responsibilities included maintaining his homes in Los Angeles, Aspen, and New York City. I would arrive a few days before he was expected and fill the house with food and flowers, making certain his every comfort was provided for. I accompanied him to restaurants, parties, meetings, and studios. The hours were long when we were together, but when he left for Europe I might have four weeks off with pay. Quite a pleasant arrangement, I must admit.

I once accompanied Donna and Giorgio to a recording session at Manhattan's "Hit Factory." Never having seen anyone record an album before, I was fascinated by the long, arduous process of combining knobs, switches, control panels, technicians, engineers, music tracks, and one very large-voiced woman to create a sound which drove masses screaming to the dance floor. Donna was extremely professional, well prepared, and ready to sing. She was very unassuming for a diva. Entertainers often have a wildly self-indulgent streak which makes their performance exciting—an arrogance which dares to say "look at me." Frequently such performers are unable to separate their on-stage persona from their off-stage personal life. That certainly proved to be true with my rock star. The real-life Donna, however, was remarkably different from the slinky, sexy seductress who sang about "bad girls" and "hot stuff." She kept a low profile in social situations, preferring the company of her family to famous faces in the crowd.

During my association with Giorgio I never saw Donna throw a "diva fit" or treat a fan rudely; if anything, she was overly accommodating. One evening she was expected at Giorgio's New York City apartment for a dinner party. The elevator man in the fashionable Central Park West building had heard from one of the porters that the Queen of Disco would arrive around 9 P.M. During his break, the excited operator rushed to a nearby record store and purchased several copies of her latest album. That evening, when Donna arrived, he asked her to sign his albums while he transported her up to Giorgio's apartment. She happily obliged, giving one of New York City's elevator operators something to talk about for years.

When the new album was completed we returned to Los Angeles, where Giorgio spent long hours mixing tracks. When he was finally satisfied with the results, he gave a dinner party for everyone who had worked so hard on the album. Donna arrived in a white silk dress and looked stunning as always. She was, and still is, a strikingly beautiful woman. After the party she asked me to walk her down the driveway to her Mercedes 450SL. She was frightened of the coyotes in the hills, which could frequently be heard howling in the night.

I looked at this tall, black "bad girl" of the dance floor, with her yards of wild hair, amazed that she could be frightened by anything.

"My goodness, Donna," I exclaimed, "you're a big, black woman, with wild hair like Methuselah. I should think the wolves would be more afraid of what *you* might do to *them*."

I could still hear her laughing as the car disappeared down the winding road.

Donna's new album featured a disco version of the music from *Evita*, the popular Andrew Lloyd Webber musical based on the life of Eva Peron. From the samples I heard I felt certain it would be a commercial success.

Surprisingly, the album was never released; I never learned why. But again, this was nothing new in Hollywood. There are vaults overflowing with completed films

149

and records that are never given a chance to find their audience.

Giorgio's mother, "Muti," was a frequent and welcome visitor. I always called her Madame, stressing the second syllable. Muti was a simple woman from the Italian mountains who probably found Los Angeles and Giorgio's life-style too overwhelming for words. She didn't speak English, which made communicating a bit of a parlor game.

Giorgio provided for his mother's every comfort. She would visit for months and stay in the adjoining guest cottage by the pool or accompany us to Aspen or New York. With his rapidly increasing wealth, Giorgio was building Muti a home in the Italian Alps. I often took her on shopping sprees along Rodeo Drive with an interpreter; several hours later we would return with a collection of designer clothes. The stylishly attired Italian mother would then accompany her son to Le Dôme or L'Orangerie for an extravagant dinner. I always admired Giorgio for the way he looked after his mother. So many people forget their families when they become successful.

When the time came for Muti's return to Italy, I carefully packed her designer wardrobe into an assortment of newly purchased Louis Vuitton luggage. Three months later she would arrive in Los Angeles wearing a simple sundress, carrying her favorite little brown canvas bag. I would pack her in the limousine and head back to Rodeo Drive to purchase an entirely new collection of clothes. Somewhere in the Italian mountains there must be closets filled with enough beautiful clothing and luggage to open a boutique.

150

* * *

Giorgio once asked me to help out at a New York party
being given by a friend of his. The event took place in the
East Side apartment of a wealthy film producer. Several
"au courant" individuals were in attendance—Francesco
Scavullo, Nanushka Manners, Andy Warhol.

While I was in the kitchen preparing for the arrival of
the guests, the Chinese houseman began preparing an
item which was not on any of the menus I had reviewed.
He began grinding a white powdery substance in a small
hand-cranked machine. Here we go again, I thought, and
began to search for the requisite sugar bowls which had
become a favorite feature at my rock star's parties. The
houseman laughed and said they wouldn't be necessary.
With several quick, deliberate strokes, he transformed
the mountain of white powder as skillfully as if he was
preparing sushi. I had to admire the result: twenty perfectly straight lines of white powder resting on a beautiful
mirrored tray. A small slot on the side contained a few
silver straws. I wondered if they were sterling, thinking
they might be difficult to polish. The houseman later
passed the tray around to guests as if he were serving
canapes. Although I had never seen this done before, I
felt it was far more civilized than setting out sugar bowls
and telling everyone to "dig in." I was thankful Giorgio
had never asked me to perform such services.

One weekend Olivier de Chandon, handsome heir to the
champagne fortune, arrived for a weekend visit at The Ice
Palace. Giorgio asked me to pick him up at the airport in
the Ferrari.

"He loves fast cars," Giorgio informed me. "If you don't mind, let him drive back."

Olivier was exiting the Air France terminal just as I pulled up. Before I had even offered, he jumped into the driver's seat and began revving the engine. I had the feeling I would make the return trip in record time. Although I'm certain they don't realize it, Californians drive in an orderly fashion compared to Europeans, who cut in and out of traffic at extremely high speeds. At the time I didn't know Olivier's favorite hobby was race car driving, but I soon learned he was extremely skilled behind the wheel. We zoomed down the freeway at breakneck speed, zigzagging between lanes. From the look of horror and anger on the other drivers' faces we were lucky no one tried to shoot us. I have always found fast cars exhilarating; La Contessa and I used to fly along Germany's Autobahn at 140 mph in her Aston Martin Lagonda.

Olivier was a great friend of Nastassja Kinski; he wanted to visit her on the set of *Cat People,* a new film for which Giorgio was composing the music. I offered to accompany him, since he was not familiar with the route to Universal Studios. We jumped into my new Fiat and began speeding down the winding road, taking corners two wheels at a time. Suddenly a police car appeared out of nowhere. Olivier pulled over and began muttering something in French. I quickly gave him my international driving license (they didn't used to have photographs). In extremely polite and impeccable English we explained that we were visitors who had misjudged the steep decline of the hill. Olivier said he was unfamiliar with sports cars and had not yet adjusted to shifting gears. Thankfully, good manners and an extremely indulgent Los Angeles policeman prevented us from getting a ticket. We continued on to our destination at a slightly slower speed.

While I was working with Giorgio, my gal-pal from London, Girly-Whirly, moved to Los Angeles. She had returned to America from her world travels and decided to settle in California for a while—which for Girly was about as long as *I* settled anywhere—two years at most. Once we were reunited we began twirling the night away at L.A.'s trendiest discotheques—Studio One, The Odyssey and Circus, Circus.

One evening we went out with La Contessa, who was in town for a few days. We piled into her six-foot-six-inch blonde escort's black Bentley Corniche and visited a few boring clubs. Looking for a bit more excitement, Sacha's friend suggested we try Circus, Circus. There were crowds of cars blocking the street, trying to get into the parking lot. In Los Angeles, however, a $200,000 car is an irresistible calling card. We passed through the crowd, pulled up to the gates, and the guards let us drive up to the entrance. La Contessa's escort tipped the two gentleman $100 each for their courtesy (and to guard the car with their lives).

The club's crowd contained a colorful mix of every possible shade on the sexual spectrum of life. Within seconds of our arrival we hit the dance floor. In our frenzy of spinning and arm flailing, I accidentally knocked a wig off the head of a rather tough-looking Spanish girl. I immediately retrieved the mop of hair and returned it to a woman in a purple fringed dress.

"Excuse me, miss. I'm terribly sorry but I believe this is yours," I said, handing over the long, red frizzy mass.

"Call me madam!" a baritone voice declared.

The Spanish woman turned out to be an East L.A. man. Girly and La Contessa began laughing at my mistake. I quickly invited the young gentleman to join us for a bottle of champagne. The last thing I wanted was to invoke the wrath of a willful, wigless Spanish transvestite.

Twenty minutes later we heard wild screams emanating from the bar area. The disc jockey began spinning one of Donna's hottest tunes. From a distance I saw a statuesque black woman with an unmistakable mass of dark hair. I dashed to the bar and just as I was about to embrace my favorite diva I heard a deep voice say, "Can you believe Miss Thing over there in those paisley print hot pants?" It was yet another transvestite who held a remarkable resemblance to the original disco queen. Girly and La Contessa offered to give me a few free lessons on how to tell the difference between the boys and the girls. It was then I realized we were in the midst of many such cross-dressers. The club must have been having a very special party. My friends teased me for the remainder of the evening; we danced until 4 A.M. and finished with breakfast in La Contessa's hotel suite.

My life with Giorgio was a non-stop journey between New York, Los Angeles, Aspen, and occasionally Munich. His considerate nature and European charm were assets which any employee could appreciate. Giorgio treated all of his associates with the greatest respect and was never abusive during even the most stressful times. Midway through the second year my grandmother became seriously ill. It had been two years since my last visit. The reality of Nansy's impending death was very disturbing; I decided to return to England indefinitely. Being close to his own mother, Giorgio could appreciate my position; he graciously accepted my resignation.

For four-and-a-half months I sat next to my grandmother's bed, watching her drift in and out of consciousness. By the fifth month, however, her condition miraculously stabilized. The doctors were amazed and I was extremely relieved. At Nansy's insistence, I returned to Los Angeles and rented a new house in the hills, the perfect place for contemplating one's future.

Eleven

While the noonday sun gently lulled me into complacency, I sipped champagne and floated aimlessly in a
circular pool. My newly rented home was nestled in the
hills of Carla Ridge, one of Los Angeles' most exclusive
cul-de-sacs. It was an elegant yet modest structure compared to the neighboring mansions, which could swallow
ten properties the size of mine and still have room for
dessert.

Despite the glorious California weather, I was feeling
very sad: I had no sooner returned to Los Angeles than
my grandmother took a turn for the worse and quietly
passed away. Some of the happiest moments in my life
had been spent in her company. I was not comforted by
the comments of well-meaning individuals who reminded me what a full life she had lived. Nansy had been
my inspiration and best friend. No matter where I was in
the world, I could always picture my grandmother sitting
in her garden and know that I belonged somewhere. With
one fleeting phone call my mental photograph was per-

manently erased; I felt empty and alone. I wished at that moment I could turn back the clock and retire to the safety and security of my childhood nursery.

The electronic purring of the poolside telephone suddenly jolted me out of my reflections. I quickly debated whether to answer the call or let the machine pick up. Feeling adventurous, I threw champagne to the wind and swam the few yards to the remote telephone.

"Hello?"

"Desmond, I can't believe you actually answered your phone. How ya doing, guy? It's—"

As soon as I heard the caller's Brooklynese voice I realized I had lost the debate. Jeffrey Archer, the head of a New York domestic employment agency, began talking faster than a Teletype. I had originally met Jeffrey when I was staffing La Contessa's Fifth Avenue apartment; ever since, he periodically telephoned with various job offers.

"—My goodness, Jeffrey, it's been such a long time!" I interrupted, trying not to become the recipient of a two-hour monologue.

I have often wondered why New Yorkers speak as if they have five minutes remaining in their lives. With the endless wave of fast-paced words I feel as if I'm being swept up into the eye of "Hurricane Chatter."

"What a surprise to hear from you!" I offered with feigned enthusiasm.

Actually I was not at all surprised. Word travels fast through the never-ending grapevine of the entertainment industry. Jungle drums could not beat out the message faster than the wagging tongues of Tinseltown. I knew that once word of my availability got around, the headhunters would soon descend for the kill.

Jeffrey immediately began to do what he did best: selling the idea that devoting oneself to serving and maintaining the life and possessions of someone else— especially a multi-millionaire—could be as "wonderful and exciting" as actually *being* that person. He told me a wealthy New York business tycoon desperately needed a majordomo to run his growing domestic empire; I was the perfect person for the job. Although I loved New York City, I had not previously thought about relocating. But Jeffrey caught me at exactly the right moment. I have often found that when tragedy strikes, or someone unexpectedly dies, we become far more flexible and willing to thrust ourselves in new directions. Nansy's death had affected me in such a way. I welcomed the opportunity to throw myself into a new challenge and, perhaps, a new life. I agreed to fly east for an interview if he would make all the necessary arrangements.

"By the way, what is the gentleman's name?" I inquired.

"Saul Steinberg," he replied.

I had never heard of him.

The next morning a first-class airline ticket arrived via express mail. I spoke briefly with Mr. Steinberg's extremely efficient secretary, Angela, and thanked her for making all of the arrangements.

I flew to New York that afternoon and checked into the Plaza Hotel. The next day I arrived at Reliance Group Holdings (Mr. Steinberg's company), at 3:15 P.M., fifteen minutes early for my appointment. I was not pleased to be kept waiting for three hours, only to be told that my appointment would have to be rescheduled for the following day. Angela was most apologetic; she appeared to be embarrassed at having to make amends for her employer's rudeness. But corporate raiders have not made their fortunes by being polite. Individuals who think nothing of putting thousands of people out of work certainly do not worry about keeping a job applicant waiting.

The next day I arrived at 8:00 A.M. for my new appointment. Ten minutes later Angela escorted me into an enormous, modernly furnished office with a panoramic view of the city. A large-framed, overweight man with a round face and horse-size teeth stepped forward to shake my hand.

"Saul Steinberg. Have a seat," he offered in a somewhat commanding tone.

I sat in an uncomfortable chair directly opposite but several inches lower than that of my prospective employer. The positioning of the furniture reminded me of a scene from *The King and I* where Anna is taught that the King must always be the tallest person in the room. While Saul began speaking, my eye focused on a photograph prominently displayed on his massive desk. The sterling silver frame showcased a very beautiful and vaguely familiar face.

He began the interview by stating that my resumé was very impressive; he had never received such glowing references before. Angela had spoken with all of my previous employers except for those who were in some remote part of the globe. The security people had conducted an investigation to make sure I wasn't an escapee from a sanatorium for deranged domestics. I was intrigued that anyone would go to such elaborate lengths before an initial interview. Based on all the evidence which had been

160

gathered, I felt certain he had already decided to offer me the job.

For the next ten minutes Saul related his personal and professional history. Once divorced, once separated (although he was desperately trying to divorce the second wife), he currently kept company with Nancy Dutiel, the Lancôme model. He swept his thick hand across her photograph like a proud eight-year-old displaying a prized baseball card. They shared thirty-four rooms in a Park Avenue duplex. He stressed the address and was most emphatic that I know it was the Rockefeller building, one of the most desirable dwellings in New York City. Years ago the apartment had contained sixty-four rooms. It was no longer feasible for anyone to own such an enormous space in Manhattan; the apartment had been divided into two smaller units. Saul and Nancy made do with thirty-four rooms; Steve Ross (CEO of Time Warner) and his wife Courtney shared the other thirty.

Like a shopkeeper listing his inventory, Saul rattled off his numerous possessions, which included a Long Island beach house in Quogue, an estate in Ocean Reef, Florida, and a vast, multi-million dollar art collection. He needed someone to run all of the residences and supervise the New York staff of twelve. Saul assured me I would be free to hire, fire, reorganize, and make whatever improvements I saw fit. As compensation for my efforts he offered a private apartment which would be decorated according to my taste, a generous salary, health insurance, and benefits. It was an extremely accommodating offer.

Saul concluded by stating that he and Nancy were flying to Paris the next day; they would be away for one week. If I was willing, I could start on Monday. He felt their absence would allow me sufficient time to familiarize myself with the apartment and staff.

"Before you make a decision, why don't you meet Nancy and check out the place," he suggested. "I'll have someone drive you over now."

Saul buzzed Angela on the intercom and told her to alert the guards and Miss Dutiel that I was on my way. He shook my hand again and told me to call him that evening with a decision.

A long black limousine crawled along the Upper East Side of Manhattan. As we approached 740 Park Avenue I glanced at my watch. Twenty blocks, twenty minutes. If only the residents spoke as slowly as the traffic moved. I gave my name to the doorman. Within minutes, a burly, gun-toting guard arrived and escorted me into the apartment. (Saul had twenty-four-hour security, not unusual for someone of his wealth and profession.)

I followed my protector down a wide gallery but stopped for a moment, starring in disbelief at a Francis Bacon triptych. Three ten-foot paintings depicted an assortment of basic body functions. I was familiar with contemporary art and could appreciate Bacon's work. But I felt that to live with pictures of someone sitting on a toilet, vomiting into a sink, and urinating into a bathtub was somewhat of a test—even for the most ardent art lover.

The guard escorted me into a darkly paneled library filled with an assortment of tapestry brocade-covered furniture. After approximately ten minutes, he returned to inform me that Miss Dutiel was not in; he wasn't sure when she would return, so I decided to leave.

The moment I walked into my hotel room Angela telephoned.

"I'm sorry for the inconvenience, but Miss Dutiel is now at home and would like to meet with you presently."

I began to feel like a yo-yo and toyed with the idea of taking the next plane back to Los Angeles. But then I heard Nansy's voice echo one of her many words for the wise: "Always explore every situation thoroughly before making any decisions."

"Angela, kindly inform Miss Dutiel I'll meet with her in one half hour, if that's convenient."

"Thank you for your patience," she replied. "I'm sure that will be fine."

As I ran out the door I had a sudden flashback of the Bacon triptych; I wondered what surprises the rest of the apartment might hold.

Thirty-five blocks and thirty-five minutes later I found myself seated in the oppressive library once again. Within moments of my arrival, Miss Dutiel swept in to greet me.

"I'm so sorry for not being able to meet with you when you first arrived. I had a fitting for a photo shoot which ran later than I expected. Please, call me Nancy."

The moment my eyes rested upon her beautiful face and figure I felt rewarded for my patience. Dressed in black leather pants with a black-and-grey checked jacket, she looked like a page out of Italian *Vogue*. As Nancy extended two graceful hands and gently pressed my palm between I recognized a faint trace of expensive perfume.

"Would you like some coffee?" she offered after we had seated ourselves on the antique sofa.

"If it's no trouble, tea would be preferable."

163

"Of course, I should have guessed," she answered as if she had failed some sort of test.

I was immediately aware of the insecure nature of this lovely young lady. She nervously fingered the strand of pearls around her neck and played with the buttons on her jacket. Nancy appeared to be as highly strung as she was beautiful.

After approximately ten minutes the butler arrived; he set the tea tray on a side table and left. Nancy began to make an effort to pour but hesitated. I think she was worried that I might scrutinize her performance. Sensing her discomfort, I offered to "play Mum" for us both. With a sigh of relief she leaned back into the sofa. I listened attentively to the Cinderella story of an Ohio farm girl magically transported into the glamorous world of high fashion. She went from bell bottoms to Balenciaga in less than a month, and eventually secured a lucrative contract with Lancôme. Her success as the mistress of a fully staffed house, however, had not been so swift: Nancy confessed that she had no idea how to run a home and would welcome my guidance and advice. I was endeared by her honesty and total lack of pretensions.

After about thirty minutes, she gave me a quick tour of the apartment. It was a magnificent space desperately in need of the vision of a single decorator. During the past decade it had been redesigned by a variety of people. In the seventies much of the apartment had been transformed by Parish Hadley; his influence was apparent. I found it quite austere, with grey velvet walls, burgundy flock paper, velvet curtains, and black lacquer furniture. The large salon was very gloomy, with an unusual assort-

164

ment of artwork: death and destruction was depicted everywhere. A Titian ("Salome with the Head of John the Baptist") pictured Salome presenting John the Baptist's severed head on a silver platter, dripping blood. In an enormous Rubens ("Adonis and the Three Graces"), hunting dogs sniffed a pool of blood surrounding Adonis' sword-impaled body while the three graces hovered in the background. Barburan's "Card Players in a Whore House" seemed quite cheerful compared to the surrounding paintings. And this was only one room, mind you. Admittedly, these were great works of art; the collection was impressive. But I felt such paintings were far more appropriate for a museum than a room where one might be entertaining guests.

The apartment featured four bedrooms, four maids' rooms, a formal dining room which could seat twenty, a full movie theatre with large leather armchairs, a breakfast room with large accompanying terrace, cavernous white-and-gray marble fireplaces, and a full games room with billiard table and slot machines. Each room, however, had been decorated in a different style.

Nancy assured me that someone was diligently working to try and update the decor; she was certain he would transform the apartment beautifully. I then saw what would be my apartment: a potentially pleasant suite of rooms which had not been refurbished since La Guardia was mayor.

When we returned to the library I thanked my hostess for the guided tour.

"I really hope you'll accept the position," she said. "As you can see I need all the help I can get."

I returned to my hotel, ordered a split of Moët, and

reviewed the last twenty-four hours. By the time I finished my second glass of champagne I had decided to accept the job. Although I had not found Saul particularly endearing, I thought Nancy was charming; she certainly would not be the type of woman to interfere. I was stimulated by the excitement of being in New York, a city which screams with energy twenty-four hours a day. I knew that working with Saul and Nancy would be challenging and, with my memories of Nansy wafting through my head, I wanted to start something new. I flew back to Los Angeles, packed my belongings, and returned to the city which would become my permanent home.

The following Monday I moved into 740 Park Avenue. I was impressed by Nancy's thoughtfulness: She had left a welcoming note and arranged to have fresh flowers placed in my room. Unfortunately, none of the household staff (except for security) had been told of my arrival. The first morning I arrived at the breakfast table with my usually cheery disposition.

"Good morning, everyone, I'm Desmond. I look forward to meeting and speaking with each of you individually. I'm certain we'll have a wonderful time working together."

The cold stares I received quickly clued me in that this was going to be an uphill battle all the way. The staff perceived me as an intruder who was going to disrupt their lives and routine. Having dealt with this type of problem before, I immediately called a meeting to sort things out. I carefully explained that I had been hired to make their lives easier; no one was in jeopardy of losing his or her job. My standards, however, were different

166

from those currently being implemented. I hoped they would understand that once we made certain improvements the apartment would be easier to maintain.

Within a week they realized I was not some English prima donna who was afraid to get his hands dirty. I firmly believe that when supervising others, you should never ask anyone to do something which you would not be willing to do yourself. Team work always produces the most desirable effect; a willingness to pitch in will always earn the respect of your fellow employees. My management approach worked wonders in ending the cold war at 740 Park.

While Saul and Nancy were away I inventoried every inch of the apartment. It was an amazing accumulation of china, silver, gold, crystal, paintings, statues, antiques, jewelry, and everything imaginable which exemplified massive wealth. For a poor boy from Brooklyn, Saul had done a remarkable job climbing the ladder of financial success.

Saul and Nancy had only just returned from Paris when we helicoptered to their 1,400-acre Cornwall, Connecticut, estate. The main house was a German schloss which had been brought over from the Rhine and rebuilt by Italian immigrants, brick by brick. It was a romantic, fantasy-like dwelling. Nancy and I worked for several months decorating a guest cottage on the estate, which was supposed to be their love nest, while the main house was being renovated. Unfortunately, the estate was sold before anyone moved in.

Nancy was a lovely woman, but very inexperienced and unsure of her position as mistress of the house. One morning, she walked into the kitchen, heated some left-over spaghetti, and ate her Italian breakfast seated upon the butcher's block—not exactly suitable behavior for a formal household. I told her that although she may have perceived her behavior as "helpful," it made the staff uncomfortable. The mistress of a fully staffed house should never venture beyond the "green door." (In formal English homes the green door separates the service area from the main part of the house; it is traditionally lined with green felt on each side to absorb the sounds and smells from the kitchen area. Saul's apartment actually had such a green felt-lined door.) I explained that the staff deserves privacy. It is unsettling if they are taking a break and the lady of the house unexpectedly waltzes in. The Europeans I had worked with couldn't even describe their kitchens. In all my years with La Contessa, I never saw her near any of her kitchens. On the yacht she once stated she didn't even know where the galley was.

My first year with the couple was quite stormy, to put it mildly. During the summer we spent weekends in Quogue. Kevin McNamara had done a beautiful job decorating Saul's beach house in a very casual yet chic English cottage style. But there was nothing casual about the atmosphere once we arrived: There were horrendous fights. The staff used to hide in the kitchen, too embarrassed to go about their duties.

One evening events escalated to such a point I had to drive Nancy to the emergency room in Southampton: She and Saul were having yet another fight at the dinner table. While she was wildly flailing her hands, Saul lost his balance and accidentally stabbed her in the hand with a dinner knife as his children looked on in horror. It quickly became apparent that these two individuals, for whatever reasons, made a potentially dangerous combination.

Several times in New York Nancy became so frustrated during her arguments with Saul that she hurled breakfast and dinner trays over the banister. I often felt sorry for the hard-working staff who had to clean up the horrid mess. On several occasions the maids were buzzed in the early morning hours to re-make the bed, which had been torn apart during an argument.

In the midst of this chaos, I diligently tried to keep things running as smoothly as possible, but it wasn't easy. I had never worked in such a turbulent environment before. I often contemplated leaving in those first months, but decided to see the challenge through. I had become very fond of Nancy and felt sorry for her. Although Saul could be rude and vulgar, he was never abusive to me. I made it clear from the beginning that I wouldn't tolerate any nonsense.

Dinner parties were often very tense situations. Saul would invite a group of business associates whom Nancy found quite boring. While he entertained his guests with a price list of all the paintings in the room, Nancy would consume more wine. She often exceeded her limit. Once she wandered away from the dinner party; I passed her in the hallway. In an extremely loud voice (which all of the guests could hear) she exclaimed, "I can't believe that tacky polyester dress that woman has on in there, can you!" During such occasions, I tried to water down her drinks with as much Perrier as possible. Although Nancy was an accomplished model in her own right, I think she felt like another one of Saul's possessions—another rare and expensive commodity. I never really understood why she stayed. She was a beautiful, financially independent woman who could have had her choice of any one of several men.

Dinner parties were a difficult time for me, watching Saul destroy a picture-perfect table with his complete lack of manners. *Spy* magazine used to call him the "Porky-Pig look-alike." He certainly had an animal-like quality when he ate, lowering his face to the plate and shoveling forkfuls of food into his mouth. Unlike Barbara in Beverly Hills, Saul was not interested in self-improvement. He believed that enormous wealth was sufficient license to excuse any kind of behavior.

Saul and Nancy's relationship quickly spiraled downhill; they agreed to end it by Labor Day. It was a difficult period for everyone while they tried to untangle their lives. When they were in the first throes of love Saul had given Nancy a precious emerald and diamond set consisting of a necklace, earrings, and bracelet. He wanted them back; Nancy refused. Worried that something might happen, she placed the valuable jewels in a safety deposit box and asked me to help her discreetly sell them at a future date.

Within a month, every trace of the beautiful young model had been removed from 740 Park. As a final blow, Nancy lost her valuable Lancôme contract to Isabella Rossellini—a woman three years her senior. She moved to the Midwest and began a much happier life. I was and still am very fond of her. She was a confused and vulnerable young woman who had become entangled in a highly destructive relationship. Nancy had a life that most girls dream about, but for a while it had turned into a nightmare.

Saul took to his new-found freedom by living the life of a swinging bachelor, dating a variety of women and partying late into the night. All of his dates were beautiful, new to the city, and impressed by his wealth. Saul, albeit not attractive in the traditional sense, became a very desirable catch for the right woman. He was rich and getting richer every day, and he was not cheap with the women he entertained. If he had a date with a young lady who didn't have the right clothes for a particular occasion, I would telephone a personal shopper at Bloomingdale's and instruct her to outfit the woman for a proper night on the town.

Saul had fun trying to impress the women with his wealth. On the first date he would send a Rolls Royce limousine to pick up his guest. After a bottle of Cristal in the main salon Saul would give a personally guided tour of the apartment, listing the purchase price of most of its contents. The evening staff stood by attired in black formal uniforms, completing the perfect picture of how the really rich supposedly live. After another glass of champagne, Saul would whisk his date out the door for an exciting night on the town: dinner at Le Cirque or La Grenouille, dancing at The Red Parrot or Le Club. It made the desired impression on these very impressionable young women.

For several months a variety of women came and went. One day, however, Saul returned from Texas with news of a new love interest. Sally Hall was a class act, with all of the necessary statistics: beauty, warmth, humor—great wealth.

Saul invited her to visit him in New York; I began massive preparations for the impending visit. The day before she was expected to arrive the telephone rang. It was the Texan beauty; I quickly introduced myself.

"It's a pleasure to speak with you," she said with the slightest trace of an accent. "I've heard so much about you I can't wait to meet you."

Saul, in trying to impress the woman, had obviously told her all about his very British majordomo.

"I won't keep you," she continued. "I just wanted to check what time Saul's plane is picking me up."

Until this moment I had heard nothing about a plane being dispatched for her arrival. I put her on hold and buzzed Saul. After I filled him in he took the call himself. Within two hours he was on his 747 en route to pick up his date.

Ms. Hall arrived with enough luggage for a three-month cruise. I immediately assigned two lady's maids to sort through the mountainous collection. Shortly after she arrived Sally graciously complimented me on the floral arrangements throughout the apartment, which consisted of her favorite flowers. Part of a majordomo's job is helping guests to feel at home. Whenever I prepared for someone's visit I would telephone secretaries, housekeepers, or personal assistants, trying to ascertain as much information as possible regarding preferences in food, flowers, alcohol, magazines, perfume, chocolates, and toiletries. The Duchess of Windsor always made sure that every guest who visited her estate had every particular item they used in their respective homes—from soap to magazines to perfume.

Many social functions had been planned during Sally's stay. The highlight was the Metropolitan Ball. This particular function is held each December and opens the New York social season of balls, galas, benefits, and grand parties. The day of the event Miss Hall realized she was missing a certain pair of Bruno Magli evening shoes which she desperately needed to complete her ensemble. Accompanied by the maids, I combed Manhattan's most exclusive stores trying to locate a duplicate pair. Five thousand dollars later, I returned with my newly purchased footwear collection only to be told that none of the choices were suitable. Finally, a private jet was dispatched to her Texas home to retrieve the forgotten shoes. They were delivered just in time for her to slip them on her feet and dash out the door. A month later, when the various shoe and plane bills arrived, I wondered if a perfect pair of pumps was really worth over ten thousand dollars.

The staff thought highly of Ms. Hall. She was cultured, polite, vivacious, warm, and quite the lady. And she rarely interfered. We all agreed she could be a good influence on Saul, who needed to be taught the mere basics of etiquette. Nothing she requested was too much trouble, because she always asked with great style. One morning she invited me to join her for tea in the library. She reiterated how much she appreciated my help and how beautifully I ran the apartment. She assured me that if she were to become a more permanent fixture in Saul's life I would have nothing to fear. Her vast social agenda precluded her from getting involved in the day-to-day running of the house. I thought it was interesting how she made an effort to reassure me the same way I had done with the staff on my first day. I knew that if Saul decided to marry Sally, she would be easy to work with and he would be better off. I lit a candle to the gods of love and hoped for the best.

It must have been a very windy day when I lit the love candle: Sally and Saul had a disagreement and ended their relationship shortly thereafter. I think it had much to do with that her wealth, independence, and sophisticated social circle intimidated Saul. At this point in time he was not part of New York society. Sally was in total control of her life and did not need to marry anyone— except for love.

Once again, the revolving door of women began to twirl with a vengeance. Saul had numerous parties, attracting a wide variety of individuals. Regular visitors included Andrew Stein and his wife Lynn Forrester, an assortment of lawyers, bankers, and even Donald Trump. Kathleen Turner arrived one evening looking absolutely delicious in a silky, slinky dress. The next day Saul instructed me to get a copy of *Body Heat,* which he watched repeatedly on the large screen of his movie theatre. He developed a boyish crush on her, but nothing came of it.

One particular evening I organized a very special dinner party. One of the female guests who attended would eventually change Saul's life, my future, and the entire New York social scene. I remembered her distinctly at the time because she had a highly unusual first name: Gayfryd.

174

Twelve

In November 1982, Saul asked me to arrange a dinner party for sixteen people which was to be followed by the screening of *Tootsie*. He told me to make it "real fancy" which in his simplified vocabulary meant as ostentatious as possible. The day of the event I worked diligently with the staff, ensuring that every last detail was perfect.

While cocktails were being served in the main salon, I made last-minute adjustments to the table setting. A beautiful but unfamiliar woman wandered into the formal dining-room and smiled at me. She was wearing a backless, strapless, salmon-colored dress which was slit so high up the front I thought I almost glimpsed her navel when she walked. This provocatively attired creature sauntered around the table until she found her designated seat. She then exchanged her placecard for the one on Saul's left and strolled out of the room. Intrigued by her sense of purpose, I decided to let the placecards fall where they may.

During dinner I watched the social engineer engage in

an obvious flirtation with my employer. Had he been one of the lamb chops we were serving for dinner she would have devoured him in a single bite. Before the white chocolate mousse arrived, Saul excused both himself and his new friend, stating that he wanted to show her a painting in another room. Dessert, coffee, brandy, and cigars had all been served, but the lesson in art appreciation was still going on. Some guests began to snicker, others laughed. When it became obvious that the newly acquainted couple had no intention of returning, the group retired to the screening room and immediately departed at the conclusion of the film.

I next saw the mystery woman the following morning at breakfast. I learned that she was Gayfryd Johnson, a New Orleans resident. Ms. Johnson would eventually receive a $1.2 million engagement ring, become Mrs. Saul Steinberg, and reign as queen of New York's nouvelle society. Art appreciation was never so lucrative.

After that infamous dinner party, life quickly changed at 740 Park. Gayfryd became Saul's obsession. For the next few months she flew from New Orleans to spend weekends with him. Although my employer was smitten with the southern femme fatale, he was never lonely during her absence. Saul was dividing his money and attention between Gayfryd and two others; all three lived out of town and were unaware of each others' existence.

Whenever any of the women came to visit, it was my job to perpetuate the fantasy that she was Saul's ''one and only.'' If Gayfryd was scheduled to arrive, I would place photographs of her in various picture frames throughout the apartment, fill vases with her favorite flowers, move her clothes into the master bedroom closets and spray the air with her chosen perfume. Ever the efficient major-domo, I kept index cards on each of Saul's girlfriends; as one left and the next arrived I would consult my notes and, with the assistance of a very amused staff, make the necessary changes. The plan was immensely successful.

One day, however, Gayfryd made an unscheduled appearance, catapulting the household staff (and Saul) into a panic. Like characters in a British farce, we swept through the apartment, frantically swapping photographs, clothing, flowers, and perfume, and finished with only minutes to spare. I thought Ms. Johnson had become aware of the household's revolving door policy and decided to put a stop to anything which might jeopardize her future.

Being an intelligent and proud woman, Gayfryd was not willing to settle for the role of the good and faithful mistress. She had ambition of epic proportions. Her personal life was in a state of disarray: Norman Johnson (her husband) had fled the country owing a fortune in back taxes (he was later discovered living a luxurious life in London); their palatial New Orleans mansion, along with most of its contents, had been confiscated, forcing Gayfryd to move into a condominium. When a woman reaches thirty and has become accustomed to the privileges which great wealth offers, it is very difficult to adjust to a simpler way of life. Saul was the perfect solution to all of her problems. Gayfryd played her trump card: she issued an ultimatum, and within weeks Saul proposed.

As striking as she is, I found her cold and unemotional. She said little but appeared to observe everything, storing bits of information for future use. She won no congeniality awards amongst the staff, who missed the days of the outgoing and gregarious Texan.

One of Gayfryd's first priorities after she permanently moved into 740 Park was to remove any trace of the other women in Saul's life. She began by throwing out everything from pots and pans to pornographic tapes. Kalif Allerton, a Los Angeles decorator, had been working on the apartment before Gayfryd's arrival. He re-did the library in crimson suede. Gayfryd hated it the moment she saw it, calling it "whore red." Because she was new, however, she didn't create a fuss. She patiently bided her time, knowing that eventually she would have her way.

Within a few months, Gayfryd was feeling more secure in her position. She decided it was time to ease in her New Orleans decorator, Tom Collum, and fire Kalif. She wanted to transform the thirty-four room duplex into a copy of what she thought was old-monied elegance: Each room was to be opulent, reflecting the palaces of another era. Although her taste certainly differed from mine, she worked very hard during the redecoration process; she eventually created an overall vision for the apartment which was a vast improvement.

Gayfryd next fired Kevin McNamara (the decorator who had been hired to work on the beach house in Quogue) and replaced him with Tom. He was a wispy Southern gentleman who had made a great deal of money, thanks to Gayfryd's choice in husbands. In addition to being her decorator, he was her confidant and occasional spy.

One day, Tom took me out to lunch and began questioning me about his favorite female. He wanted to find out what I thought it would be like once Gayfryd married

Saul and officially became mistress of the household. I felt he was acting upon the soon-to-be Mrs. Steinberg's instructions, trying to gather more bits of information. Whenever Tom complimented his New Orleans pal, I simply bit my tongue and nodded in agreement.

We spent the summer in Quogue, during which time Gayfryd asked me to find additional staff for the beach house. We had two Spanish maids in residence who were sisters. In addition to working in Quogue, the women also helped out in New York. Gayfryd instructed me to fire one of the sisters because she didn't speak English. I begrudgingly complied with her request; shortly thereafter, the other sister was also fired. We constantly had help coming and going as Gayfryd set about re-staffing both the beach house and the New York apartment. This is not unusual when a new woman arrives on the scene. Like a newly inaugurated president, a new Fifth or Park Avenue wife will generally "clean house," hiring an entirely new staff if possible. This gives her greater control. No one is privileged to information about the household or her husband which she, herself, does not have. I waited to see how I would fit in (or out of) Gayfryd's plans.

Saul had a habit of recycling jewelry. A particularly amusing incident occurred involving a Cartier tennis bracelet. The $10,000 diamond bracelet had originally been given to Sally Hall. The Texan, however, gave it back when she decided Saul was not the man of her dreams. Saul next gave it to a female entrepreneur he was trying to impress. She was a lovely woman, but as she never intended to marry Saul, she too returned the brace-

179

let. The recycled diamonds eventually found a permanent home in Gayfryd's jewelry case, which she kept in Saul's bedroom.

One evening the female entrepreneur attended a dinner party while Gayfryd was in New Orleans. Midway through the evening, she wandered upstairs into the master suite. When she discovered Gayfryd's jewelry case she couldn't resist temptation; she was amused to discover that the Cartier hand-me-down had found yet another home. The feisty female then returned to the party and mischievously announced "Saul, I see you've given *my* jewelry to *Gayfryd!* How gauche!"

In August of 1983, I was seriously ill and had to be hospitalized for a month. After being released I recuperated for six weeks at home. During this period Gayfryd continually telephoned, trying to find out when I was going to be well enough to return to work. By this point I felt that she eventually wanted me out of the apartment, but she was not yet ready to run the show by herself. She was in the early stages of her take-over attempt and needed my assistance.

Saul and Gayfryd went on a trip to the Orient in the fall of '83. Whenever Saul went on vacation he seldom called in. Gayfryd, by contrast, telephoned frequently with what she deemed to be "important" requests. While they were in Hong Kong, she telephoned to ask if I had ordered the laundry hampers for the beach house in Quogue. I found it odd that her mind was on laundry, particularly since the beach house wouldn't be in use for another six months. She often telephoned from exotic locations with similarly "urgent" requests.

When Gayfryd returned from the trip she began her transformation into a proper Jewess. She knew that her being a Gentile was a strike against her—especially with Saul's family. Although she was not overly fond of her future relatives, she wanted to endear herself to them as much as possible; she began receiving instruction from a rabbi. Gayfryd worked very hard to become a caring, devoted, soon-to-be Jewess—a woman who once said she adored Saul "for his mind." Since I had seen him in his bathing suit, I could appreciate the comment. Only two small problems stood in the way: her husband and his wife. Saul's second wife would only agree to divorce him for $10 million; Gayfryd had a husband in prison who was not being overly cooperative with her divorce proceedings.

During this period, Gayfryd relocated her mother and father from New Orleans to a house in New Jersey. They were constantly at the apartment, ensuring that Gayfryd had a back-up team in case anything flared up. With her mother at her side, Gayfryd frequently tried to give the chef cooking tips. He felt her level of culinary sophistication was very limited and that all she needed was "a little woman to come in and throw things together." Their difference in cooking styles eventually came to a head when Gayfryd ordered the four-star chef to prepare her recipe for chicken casserole, which basically consisted of frying a chicken and then smothering it with a can of Campbell's soup. The chef, far from amused by her home-style cuisine, refused to cook the casserole. Although the gentleman had been preparing Saul's meals for over five years, he was terminated within two weeks without any notice or severance pay.

*　*　*

When I first went to work for Saul he had a talented and charming florist who came to the apartment twice a week, filling the huge duplex with magnificent arrangements. He was quite popular with the residents of both Fifth and Park avenues. The florist continued after Gayfryd's arrival, but she disliked him from the beginning. Gayfryd was not fond of anyone who had had any dealings with Nancy, Saul's previous long-term girlfriend. She felt that anyone who had worked with the beautiful model was privileged to information she didn't have, and such information could give the other person the upper hand. She tolerated the florist only until she was secure enough in her position to fire him.

Thanksgiving '83 Gayfryd gave a party for Saul's family. It was also the day they were announcing their upcoming marriage, so she wanted everything to be perfect. The day before Thanksgiving the florist prepared lovely holiday arrangements on the large dining-room table. Gayfryd arrived to inspect his work and instantly hated it. While he quietly stood by she began dismantling the centerpieces, throwing unwanted decorations on the floor. The florist was not pleased and quickly departed.

Shortly after the engagement party, Saul telephoned me from the office and told me that because he and Gayfryd were now officially engaged I should make an effort to collaborate with her in all matters relating to the running of the household. I could see the writing on the wall; while I was prepared to work with her to the best of my abilities, I had a difficult time with her definition of the word "collaborate."

One month later, the same florist arrived to decorate

182

the apartment for Christmas. With the assistance of several helpers, he began to lay out his materials and bedeck the house in the same traditional style he had done in previous years. While he was working, I received a telephone call from Saul's plane. Gayfryd wanted to inform me that she had hired another florist; I should fire the gentleman we were currently using. I tried to explain that the florist was already working in the apartment but she said, "Get rid of him."

I executed her instructions and the florist, once again, quickly departed. He did, however, charge Saul a tidy sum for Gayfryd's bad manners. I later learned he also shared the story with a majority of his Fifth and Park Avenue customers. Shortly thereafter, Gayfryd instructed Saul to fire the florist from his four-year position of arranging the flowers for Saul's office.

During Christmas, Saul and Gayfryd and their respective families vacationed in Ocean Reef, Florida. A few days before the holiday, Gayfryd's lawyer telephoned to inform her that the divorce had finally gone through. Saul had already finalized his divorce by agreeing to pay his wife several million dollars. They were both finally free to be married. Gayfryd told Saul she wanted to get married immediately in case Norman decided to contest the divorce decree. She was terrified her ex-husband would still try to prevent her from becoming Mrs. Steinberg.

The very next day they rushed off to be married by a ship's captain at the Ocean Reef Club. Of course, Gayfryd made sure the financially rewarding pre-nuptial agreement was Federal Expressed to Florida for her and Saul's signature before she actually said, "I do." Several days after the ceremony there were many heated discussions

183

about whether the marriage was valid. Gayfryd spoke to a lawyer, trying to ascertain whether there was a Louisiana law that a divorce was not final until thirty days after it had been decreed.

To ensure their marriage was legal, and to provide their friends and relatives a chance to celebrate the union, thirty days later Saul and Gayfryd had a second marriage ceremony at the Central Synagogue on Lexington Avenue. Several people found it quite shocking that even though this was Gayfryd's third marriage and she was pregnant, she still wore a white dress.

At the synagogue her mother told me, "This is the third wedding of hers I have been to and *this* is *enough!* I don't want to go to any more of Gayfryd's weddings."

Mrs. McNab was not pleased that her daughter had converted to Judaism, forsaking her own family background. She said, "It will be over my dead body that they change my grandchild's religion. Especially after they told him that his father was dead!" She was referring to Rayne, the son Gayfryd had had with Norman. Apparently, when Norman was imprisoned for tax evasion, Gayfryd told the child his father was dead. Sadly, her statements proved true when Norman jumped off of a Houston building following his release from prison.

Now that Gayfryd was legally married to Saul, she felt secure in her position despite some criticism she was receiving from New York's old-monied society. This was apparent from some of the comments she made at the time. One morning, shortly after their second marriage ceremony, she drew me aside and said, "We *are* one of the richer families in New York, so people will *learn* to accept me." I just smiled and continued with my work.

184

Another time, when we were discussing her decorating plans, I told Gayfryd that unlike her, Saul was not fond of flowered fabrics and chintz. She simply smiled at me and said, "Saul will learn to love flowered fabrics."

Within less than a year Gayfryd had transformed herself into a "10021" wife. Faster (socially) than a speeding Ferrari, more powerful (politically) than the men they marry, able to empty expensive stores in a single day, these women are far more frightening than anything located in Stepford.

10021 is New York City's most exclusive zip code. If Los Angeles has its platinum triangle, then New York has its jewel-encrusted rectangle—each area so named because of its residents' financial status. The rectangle is comprised of the blocks between Sixtieth and Eighty-sixth streets on Manhattan's East Side, bordered by Fifth and Park avenues on either side.

The majority of the 10021 wives I met during this period were all part of a growing group of females referred to as "the second wife": women who secure their financial futures by attaching themselves to highly successful businessmen. With finely woven pre-nuptial agreements providing the golden thread, it is not uncommon for some of these wives to receive up to one million dollars for each year they are able to endure their new-found matrimonial bliss—quite a good salary by anyone's standards.

The entrepreneurs they marry are usually aging, ill-mannered, arrogant businessmen who no longer require the services of a devoted wife and mother. Instead, the men are searching for a combination mistress/public rela-

185

tions person. These second wives, who are often as much as twenty years younger and twenty inches taller than their spouses, all share the "X-factor": They are usually ex-models, ex-stewardesses, ex-wives, or ex-working girls of one sort or another. Anorexically thin, surgically preserved, and expensively clad, these women are all striving to be crowned queen of their own self-created society.

And what are the qualifications for becoming a 10021 wife? Unlike in your average beauty pageant, there is no swimsuit competition. There is, however, a designer evening gown category where the average dress can be had for a mere $15,000. Only a handful of designers, however, are acceptable. In addition, it is advisable to have your dressmaker to dinner at least once a month or pose with him for commercial advertisements to help promote his clothing—like Gayfryd and her Fifth Avenue friends did with Arnold Scaasi in the "Me and My Scaasi" campaign. I often wondered if such advertisements would start a trend: These women could pose with all the men in their lives who served them so well. Imagine, "Me and My Hairdresser," "Me and My Plastic Surgeon," or even "Me and My Majordomo."

Potential candidates must score high marks in the talent competition before becoming a 10021 wife. The contestants must be clever in capturing their prey, masters in the art of conspicuous consumption (but thrifty when the expense is not self-related), strict authoritarians when it comes to dealing with the household staff, secure in their newly acquired self-importance, and very creative when it comes to doing whatever is necessary to rise to the top

186

of the social ranks. In the world of the 10021 wives, Gayfryd set the definitive example.

The new Mrs. Steinberg and I frequently differed on management technique. I preferred one based on trust; she preferred one based on humiliation. Gayfryd would not allow any of the staff members to lock the doors to their rooms. Eventually, I found out why: When they were out, she would enter the tiny maids' rooms and search through their closets. If the rooms were untidy she would chastise the girls for their slovenliness. Not one to trust the competency level of her staff, Gayfryd would hide various items behind curtains and under furniture and then check later in the day to see if the maids had cleaned properly and removed the hidden items. I had been supervising domestics for years but had never encountered such dehumanizing tactics.

Like a true 10021 wife, Gayfryd knew how to be thrifty when the expense was not self-related. Although she thought nothing of spending $8,000 for a set of Porthault bed linens or $3,500 for a single Flora Danica china place setting from Tiffany's, she found ways of trimming other expenditures which she deemed unnecessary. Before her arrival the staff used to have a cooked lunch every day. Gayfryd quickly put a stop to this extravagance and said, "Let them eat sandwiches." In addition, she told the maids that they were allowed to take only one yogurt per day from the refrigerator. Gayfryd would count the yogurts each day to ensure that the maids abided by her wishes. If they exceeded their daily allowance, she would berate them for their greed.

*   *   *

In February of '84 I decided that I was going to marry a ballerina that I had known for a very long time. I met Sally, known fondly as Swan Forever Regal (SFR), at a benefit for a dance workshop. She was a Balanchine girl—a beautiful ballerina characterized by a tall, graceful stature and a swan-like neck. I found her to be quite captivating, witty, magical, and serene. Her manners and mannerisms were those of a lady.

Sally was suddenly thrust into my madcap life of parties, dinners, and nights on the town. Of course all of this had to be squeezed into Saul and Gayfryd's schedule. It wasn't easy, but I was determined. After Nansy's death I tried to begin to create a life for myself outside of my job. Sally and I traveled to tropical places; she had sat at my bedside when I had been hospitalized for a month.

We celebrated our engagement at a black-tie party given by a close society friend of Sally's; we exchanged vows on February 7, 1984. SFR was the most wonderful, kind, loyal, and loving woman I had ever met. We had a fairy-tale romance.

Saul and Gayfryd learned of my marriage plans when I sent them an invitation to the engagement party. They were unable to attend and never sent any type of engagement or wedding present. When Gayfryd initially found out that I was getting married, she was not pleased. She called me into the library and said, "Well, this is very inconvenient that you should be getting married. What about us? Our needs?" I gathered there and then that no one was supposed to have any life of his own.

*   *   *

188

A few days after Labor Day in 1984 Gayfryd gave birth to a beautiful baby girl: Holden Gayfryd Steinberg. I hired a proper British nanny from London who had trained at Norland. Two weeks after giving birth, Gayfryd, along with Saul, went to The Pritikin Institute in California for six weeks so she could work herself back into shape. Saul, alas, returned the same as ever.

During the period Saul and Gayfryd were at the health spa, my wife stayed over at 740 Park Avenue a few times. At this point, I was maintaining a residence in Saul and Gayfryd's apartment and a separate residence with my wife. When Gayfryd returned and found out that my wife had occasionally stayed with me at the apartment, she was not pleased. (Her mother had obviously provided her with a detailed report on the day-to-day occurrences in the household.) Gayfryd said my behavior was improper and set a bad example. (My mind suddenly flashed to that infamous dinner party when Gayfryd first met Saul.) I replied, "I sincerely doubt it sets a bad example if you are married to the person you are sleeping with. Really, Gayfryd, if you can't sleep with your own wife who are you supposed to sleep with?"

As the months went by it became increasingly apparent that Gayfryd wanted to be sole manageress of the household. She was capable and hard-working; she really didn't need my help. And being the majordomo, I knew too many secrets about Saul's past. After tolerating several months of her undermining my authority, I finally confronted both Saul and Gayfryd in their bedroom one evening. I politely said that since Gayfryd would like to

189

be the majordomo of the house I would be happy to resign my position.

Gayfryd looked a little shocked by my comments.

Saul, who knew how well I managed everything and was always pleased with my work, said, "Gayfryd, do you really want to do all the duties Desmond does so well?"

She innocently replied, "Oh, no, darling. I could never do things as well as Desmond." She felt that I was being overly sensitive; she never meant to imply that she wanted to replace me. After a polite little speech worthy of an Academy Award, she declared the matter closed.

The matter, however, was far from closed. Early the next day, Gayfryd summoned me to the morning room. She looked me straight in the eye and exclaimed, "How *dare* you say something like that in front of Saul! You may have won this round, but I'll get my way in the end. I always do!"

I left the Steinbergs shortly thereafter. It was clear that Gayfryd wanted to be in charge; and as Saul's new wife, she certainly had every right. I think she was an independent woman who wanted to prove what a good wife, mother, housekeeper, and partner she could be. She did improve Saul's life in certain areas. But I found the calculating manner in which she went about getting what she wanted unconscionable.

After I left, Gayfryd carved out a niche for herself in nouvelle society. During the eighties she was constantly being written about in all of the social columns. She became quite infamous for the extravagant parties she gave. Her organization of the 1988 wedding between

Saul's daughter, Laura, and Jonathan Tisch at New York's Metropolitan Museum of Art was rumored to have cost in excess of $3 million.

In 1989, Gayfryd finally went too far; her socially extravagant efforts stirred a great debate in the national press. She planned, executed, and paid for Saul's fiftieth birthday party, an event which was billed as "An Evening of Seventeenth Century Old Masters in Celebration of Saul's Fiftieth Year." The gala, which cost hundreds of thousands of dollars, featured a re-creation of a seventeenth-century Flemish eating–drinking house; Oriental rugs thrown over the grass to ensure that guests' feet remained dry; identical twins dressed as mermaids in the swimming pool; and ten enormous "tableaux vivants"— live actors in poses re-creating Old Masters paintings. One model received more than her share of attention by posing naked for a living re-creation of Rembrandt's "Danae."

Saul was overwhelmed with his wife's efforts and reportedly said, "This may be a bit of history. Honey, if this moment were a stock, I'd short it." Gayfryd defended her enthusiastic efforts by stating, "My mother always says, 'Don't tell people you love them; show them!' And this is my way of saying, 'I love you.' "

Ever since Gayfryd gave her husband the supposedly $1 million birthday card, she has kept an extremely low profile.

Thirteen

After my unpleasant experience with the Steinbergs I thought about returning to Europe. I was not endeared to this mutated species in which excessive wealth suddenly transformed employers into self-proclaimed gods. Having been raised in an environment characterized by good manners, I didn't think I could adjust to the change in rules.

When I compared my grandmother's management style to Gayfryd Steinberg's, I shuddered. These nouveau riche individuals made it hard enough to *perform* one's job—let alone take *pride* in it. And it is exactly that quality I find lacking in the majority of today's work force. The ability to take pride in what we do allows us to perform our work each day to the best of our abilities. Sadly, many jobs have been reduced to nothing more than an exchange: so many hours of labor for so much money. I frequently encounter apathetic workers from all walks of life who are not willing to take that extra step which separates a job from a job well done.

I take great pride in creating a perfect table setting or researching expected guests' preferences to make them feel at home. But if those efforts are never acknowledged, it becomes increasingly difficult to maintain a commitment and enthusiasm for the task at hand. After a certain point, money is *not* reward enough. Everyone—even a Saul Steinberg—needs a word of encouragement or a pat on the back for a job well done.

The ''10021'' employers I encountered rarely acknowledged the positive accomplishments of their employees. Rather, they thrived on accentuating the negative as a means of elevating their status even higher. As a result, employees become indifferent; job performances reflect accordingly. If you feel you're going to be criticized or ignored no matter how hard you try, eventually you stop trying.

I have heard many a ''10021'' or Beverly Hills wife utter, ''It's impossible to find good help anymore!'' I believe it's (almost) impossible to find good employers anymore. The two go hand-in-hand; one feeds the other.

My grandmother used to say, ''If you don't wake up in the morning with a sense of enthusiasm for your job— look for a new job.'' Unfortunately it is not that simple; many people have family and financial commitments which do not permit them to freely make changes. The challenge then becomes trying to make the position more palatable. But when you reach the point where that is no longer possible, it becomes imperative to move on as quickly as possible—no matter how difficult that may be.

As has always been the case in my life, it was only a matter of time before a phone call or a dinner party invitation would thrust me in a new direction. Jeffrey Archer, the gentleman at the domestic employment agency who had led me to the Steinbergs, telephoned once again. I was ready to hang up, based on his last recommendation, but Jeffrey was very accomplished in his work; he dangled the bait and before I knew it I had agreed to meet an extremely wealthy Wall Street financier who was supposedly "desperate" to meet me.

The following afternoon at precisely 3 P.M. I walked into an ultra modern Fifth Avenue office to greet the perspective employer. Asher Edelman, like Saul, had earned his reputation and fortune through the art of buying and selling companies. The moment I shook his well-manicured hand, however, I realized he couldn't have been more different from Saul Steinberg. Well-tanned and handsome with a muscular physique, he looked more like an actor on a press junket than a corporate raider in the midst of a multi-million-dollar deal. From the furniture in his office to the clothing on his back, Asher exemplified style unlike any other gentleman I have ever met. (He supposedly inspired the Gordon Gekko character portrayed by Michael Douglas in *Wall Street*.)

Apparently we had spoken once when his daughters were invited to a party at the Steinbergs'. Asher explained that he had heard wonderful things about my abilities and knew I was the majordomo for him. He laughed and told me he had heard many of the Gayfryd stories; he was certain it was only a matter of time before I left. I was surprised when he mentioned that he had been to school with Saul. For a man in his mid-forties, Asher looked incredibly youthful. It's amazing what hundreds of millions of dollars can do to improve the quality of one's skin.

Like his many predecessors, Asher quickly listed his major acquisitions: a 10,000-square-foot Manhattan apartment; a country house in Woodstock, New York; a ski lodge in Sun Valley, Idaho; and a 120-foot luxury yacht. He had been married to the same woman for eighteen years; together they had adopted three girls. One of his greatest accomplishments was an extensive collection of contemporary art which included the works of Picasso, Miró, Stella, and Schnabel.

Asher offered me a live-out position, five days per week, eight hours per day, unless there were parties or out-of-town travel. Compared to some of my previous positions, it sounded like a part-time job. I welcomed a less demanding schedule because my personal life was in a state of upheaval: I had begun renovations on a loft in Tribeca and had recently divorced my wife of two years. Like many modern-day fairy tales, the challenge of juggling two high-pressured careers precluded a happy ending. Sally now worked in the crazy world of television; I worked in the even crazier world of the very rich. Our schedules became totally incompatible. The pressures of dealing with our jobs often crept into our homelife. We saw less and less of each other; when we did, one of us was usually asleep. Our problem was not unique. But after two years of communicating through yellow Post-its attached to the refrigerator we agreed to end our marriage amicably.

After explaining a few details about how he liked to work, Asher concluded the interview by offering me a very generous salary. I accepted and agreed to start the following week.

I walked away from the meeting exhilarated—something I hadn't felt for quite some time. Asher reminded me of Giorgio; he was very European and sophisticated. I remember hearing Nansy's voice saying "every cloud has a silver lining." (Her endless list of sayings has haunted me throughout my life.) This next period of my career—with the few odd exceptions—was enjoyable; my work was, once again, stimulating and fun. I had time for my life and Asher proved to be a courteous, understanding, and appreciative employer.

The first time I stepped foot into 120 East End Avenue I felt that sense of wonder and amazement one has when viewing a great work of art. When I think back on all of the apartments, houses, villas, and châteaux I have visited throughout the world, Asher's apartment is by far the most stunning example of contemporary design I have ever seen. Much of the credit goes to the imaginative work of Tod Williams and Billie Tsien, the husband-and-wife architectural team. They did an impressive job gutting four apartments and creating an enormous loft-like space of exquisite style. Everything—from telephones to entire rooms—was hidden behind sliding panels. With the push of a button an otherwise invisible compartment in the wall suddenly opened and a telephone appeared. Other buttons made entire walls vanish, revealing an expansive art gallery, a study, or a discotheque, depending on which button you pressed. It was a masterpiece of design work.

Magnificent works of contemporary art were exhibited throughout the apartment. A Schnabel creation of broken dishes and one of Chamberlain's crushed car sculptures were both prominently displayed in the dining room. The table was constructed in glass and metal; the base had been painted vibrant shades of orange, purple, green, red, blue, and yellow. Eighteen Bentwood chairs, each painted to match a particular color in the base, surrounded the table, which rested upon a whimsical carpet of green Astroturf. It certainly wouldn't suit everyone's taste, but I loved it. Asher commissioned an artist to create a set of oversized forks, knives, and spoons with large faux jewels set into the handles. I was frequently amused watching first-time dinner guests maneuver the colossal cutlery.

The one-thousand-square-foot art gallery featured a magnificent sphere-themed Stella. The drawing room had been decorated entirely in white, except for a black Steinway grand piano and a floor-to-ceiling Miró triptych covering two walls. The Miró had a mirrored panel in the middle which reflected the entire room. Eight sets of French windows opened onto a terrace overlooking the park and the East River. It was one of the lightest, brightest apartments I had ever seen.

When I arrived, Asher's wife, Penny, escorted me through a maze of passageways to her study. Penny was one of those extremely intelligent and articulate individuals who had a difficult time communicating with anyone she presumed to be below her intelligence level. She preferred those people who could quickly pick up on what she was saying before she had to explain herself. From the first few minutes of our conversation I presumed most of her friends were clairvoyant. During my initial interview Asher had mentioned that Penny traveled frequently. I decided to ignore her attitude, as I had done so many times in the past with other employers.

Penny wanted me to arrive each day by 7:30 A.M. The chaos created by three children, three nannies, two housemen, a chauffeur, laundress, and cook was more than she could handle. She wanted someone to help organize and supervise the morning routine. I agreed to arrive early if I could leave by 4 P.M.—unless there were parties. Penny said that wouldn't be a problem since they were out most evenings. I assumed that she meant she and Asher were out *together,* but I soon learned this was not the case. They led totally separate lives except for special occasions and holidays.

Within weeks I was driving to their Woodstock house for the Thanksgiving holiday. Everyone arrived separately: Penny in her Porsche; Asher in his Mercedes accompanied by a butler, chauffeur, and guard; the children, staff, and supplies followed in jeeps and wagons.

I got my first taste of family life during our stay at their large colonial country house. Asher was his usual charming self, but Penny could be difficult and moody. I think being in such close proximity to her husband for several days was a challenge.

We survived the weekend and returned to the city. Penny immediately departed for Sun Valley; I didn't see her again until we were "en famille" at Christmas. I was not required to work holidays, but, as December 25 rapidly approached, Asher asked if I would accompany him to Sun Valley. If I was amenable he would give me ten days off over New Year's while he vacationed in Brazil. Asher was very smart about getting what he wanted: He always asked in a very polite manner and offered some reward in return, which made it difficult to turn him down. I agreed to spend Christmas in Sun Valley.

We left on his private jet with the usual entourage of children, nannies, cook, and housekeeper. I sat in the front of the plane with Asher, which allowed us the opportunity to talk privately. He told me (as I had suspected) that he had a girlfriend—a Brazilian beauty named Regina—and that he and Penny had an "understanding." He reaffirmed that I was working for *him* and to try not to take anything Penny said or did personally.

Although it was the Christmas holiday, Asher worked non-stop. Our days began very early: He liked to be dressed and on the telephone to his office by 5:30 A.M. I happily obliged, as I was looking forward to my forthcoming vacation. I had only been with him eight weeks, so I was trying to be as accommodating as possible. The festivities proceeded without any unusual occurrences; Penny was actually quite pleasant. Asher surprised me with a large bonus at 6 A.M. on Christmas morning. During the time I had worked for Saul, neither I nor any of his other employees had ever received a bonus of any kind. Asher's continual acknowledgment of my performance encouraged me to make every effort to ensure that his life ran smoothly.

We returned to New York and on December 28 I packed Asher's suitcases and sent him on his way to Rio to meet with his Brazilian beauty. I departed the next day for London to visit my mother for the New Year.

While I was working with Asher I was able to hire two of the employees whom Gayfryd had fired. When Asher needed a gourmet chef, I hired the gentleman who was given his walking papers because he refused to cook Gayfryd's recipe for chicken casserole. I was happy to offer him a job after he lost his previous one under such unpleasant circumstances. He catered luncheons in Asher's office, traveled with us on holidays, and transformed ordinary dinner parties into culinary events. He was one of the most talented and imaginative chefs I have ever known, and Asher was more than happy with his work.

I also hired the florist Gayfryd had me fire during Christmas. Bertram created beautiful arrangements in Asher's sumptuous apartment. On one occasion he truly surpassed himself. Asher and Penny (this was one of their few joint ventures) held a lovely dinner party on Halloween for a foreign ballet company which was touring America. I arranged ten round tables in the gallery and covered them in bright cloths. Bertram colored pumpkins in an assortment of luminous paints. After carving a variety of expressions in the faces of the pumpkins he placed small candles inside to bring them to life. The food was arranged like a roman banquet on the large dining room table. A disc jockey from one of New York's hottest clubs spun the latest records in Asher's discotheque. It was a wonderful evening, and Asher was most appreciative of our hard work and imaginative ideas.

Dinner parties were always a great cause for celebration. With a staff of seven to share the work, we could easily serve eighteen at a sit-down dinner without a fuss. Asher was unique in that he didn't socialize a great deal with the "10021" crowd. Most of his friends were people like Divine and Diane Brill. It was very much a chic downtown crowd characterized by gorgeous Brazilian models who poured themselves into skin-tight leather dresses. The stereo system pumped high-volume disco while the eclectic crowd danced to a beat not normally heard on the Upper East Side. In Latin style, most of the dinners did not begin until 9 P.M. No matter how late they went, however, Asher was always up by 5:30 A.M. to start his day. Wall Street waits for no man.

When Penny was out of town, Asher's increasingly steady girlfriend Regina frequently moved in. Regina was a Brazilian socialite who had been educated in Europe. With raven hair, chiseled features, and long shapely legs, she carried herself like a true aristocrat. Glamorous, chic, and expensive clothing showcased a well-toned body. Regina was every bit Asher's equal in style. The household staff sometimes found her overly confident air intimidating. I thought she was the kind of woman who seemed to have everything going for her—looks, background, money, love—and knew it.

Regina had her own apartment off Park Avenue where Asher would stay if Penny was in town. No matter where he slept, however, he was always back in his apartment by 6 A.M. to have breakfast with the children. If Regina stayed in Asher's apartment, she kept out of sight until the children were packed off to school. She spent an entire year coming and going from the apartment before the youngsters even met her. I respected them all for considering the children and acting discreetly.

One particular luncheon, Penny was out of town and Regina played hostess. I was helping the houseman rearrange furniture in the library. As per Asher's instructions, I placed a carefully ironed white linen tablecloth on the buffet table. Regina, who had a fiery Brazilian temper, stormed into the room, interrupted my conversation with Asher, and began an argument over the cloth. She hated it and felt it was inappropriate for the occasion. To illustrate her point, she grabbed the white linen, yanked it off the table, and with a matador's flourish, tossed it on the floor. Asher looked shocked; I was horrified.

"Regina!" exclaimed Asher. "Desmond just saw Gayfryd Steinberg's head on your shoulders! Someone just spent two hours ironing that. You have no right to behave like a spoiled child in my apartment."

They quickly adjourned their argument into the next room. I had to commend Asher for his sense of humor and for pointing out and acknowledging the work of his household staff—even at the expense of incurring his mistress' wrath.

It was only a matter of time before Regina gave Asher an ultimatum: either he divorce Penny and marry her or he could say "goodbye to Rio." Being a mistress is not as prosperous or respectable as being a wife. A smart woman will only play the role for so long before moving on to better prospects. Regina was an intelligent, sophisticated, and beautiful woman; she wasn't going to waste her time settling for second best.

Asher agreed to divorce Penny, who had happily put up with their "arrangement" for several years; although they no longer behaved as husband and wife, they were, nevertheless, still friends. But Penny was far from thrilled at the thought of a divorce; the usually quiet Mrs. Edelman suddenly became quite boisterous. Asher paid handsomely for the privilege of making Regina his wife.

Penny received a large apartment on Central Park West, the houses in Sun Valley and Woodstock, plus an enormous cash settlement. Since she had been with Asher for eighteen years, it was only fair that she share in the fruits of his success. During those years, Penny had become privy to very privileged information; Asher certainly did not want her as an enemy. Consequently, they divorced quietly and amicably.

Before the divorce was finalized, Asher and Penny spent another Christmas in Sun Valley for the children's sake. Once again, they made every possible effort to make their daughters feel as secure as possible. It was a tense but tolerable situation. A few days before Christmas, Asher hurt his back skiing and was in considerable pain. I had two options for transporting him to the doctor's office: Asher's jeep or Penny's wagon. I felt the comfort of the wagon was the more desirable choice under the circumstances. As soon as Penny returned from shopping I told her of Asher's plight.

"Oh, dear. How unfortunate," she replied. "I wish I could help but I've got an appointment."

She immediately departed for the health club, leaving me to drive Asher in a bumpy jeep to the doctor's office. For the rest of the holiday she went about her affairs while Asher lay in pain.

When Penny returned to New York, I helped her pack her clothing and personal possessions which were then transferred to the new apartment across town. Regina permanently moved into Asher's apartment; she didn't waste any time in asserting her authority. She was an aggressive woman with her own vision of how everything should be done. Unlike Penny, Regina wanted to become actively involved in the day-to-day running of the house, which was characteristic of a second wife.

Having learned from my experience when Gayfryd married Saul, I knew it was time to move on before a showdown began. Although I was not particularly endeared to Regina, we enjoyed an amicable relationship. I had no desire to wait until we became enemies.

I happily resigned my position and told Asher that I was contemplating returning to Europe to spend more time with my family. He was most kind and wished me the best of luck.

Asher married Regina shortly thereafter. Several years later they moved to Lausanne, Switzerland. Asher, a lover and supporter of art all his life, finally saw one of his dreams realized: Musée d'Art Contemporain, Foundation Asher Edelman—Switzerland's first important contemporary art museum, which showcases Asher's $100 million art collection.

As luck would have it, however, I never made it back to Europe. While I was once again contemplating my move, I heard of a high-profile couple in the entertainment industry who were looking for a majordomo. My friends said I had to apply for the job; they were certain it would prove to be the most exciting working experience of my life. Although I didn't know it at the time, my next job would irrevocably change my life.

Fourteen

News travels fast through the social circles of New York, and so do job opportunities. One evening in 1986, while dining with friends, I learned that Phil Donahue and Marlo Thomas were looking for a majordomo to manage their newly renovated New York City apartment. After making a few inquiries, I finally reached Phil's secretary at NBC. She directed me to Marlo's secretary, Billie, who confirmed that the position was still open and who then scheduled a preliminary interview. I must confess, at this time I was only familiar with Phil Donahue. I had seen his talk show, but I had never heard of Marlo Thomas. I was born and raised in London; to my knowledge, *That Girl* was never televised in England. I thought perhaps she was a florist because I remembered reading an article in *New York* magazine about a very expensive florist called Marlo. I soon learned, however, that Marlo the florist was definitely not "That Girl."

My preliminary interview with Billie went extremely well. Although I found Miss Thomas' secretary lacking in certain social skills, she was, nevertheless, professional; Billie arranged for me to meet with Miss Thomas at her Fifth Avenue penthouse.

The day of the interview, I awoke at 6:30 A.M. to allow myself enough time to properly prepare for the 10 A.M. appointment. I dressed in a crisp white shirt, bow tie, and black suit, remembering what my grandmother had always said about first appearances: "Present yourself to the world as you wish the world to see you, as surely, by this, you will be judged." Since it was a freezing morning and a snowstorm had just passed, I wanted to wear my fur coat, but was unsure whether it would be appropriate. I had done some research on Miss Thomas and had discovered that she was a vocal advocate and activist for various human rights organizations. I thought she also might have been an antifur activist, and I did not want to offend her before our interview had even begun. After debating the "to fur or not to fur" question for several minutes, I finally settled on a black cashmere overcoat and quickly departed.

I arrived at the Thomas–Donahue Fifth Avenue apartment at precisely 10 A.M. Billie took my overcoat and opened the closet door, revealing what looked like dozens of furs in a variety of species. I was dumbfounded and feared that my lone cashmere would be devoured by the surrounding animals. As I walked into the drawing room of the newly remodeled penthouse, I was immediately taken aback by the floor-to-ceiling windows that lined the Fifth Avenue side of the apartment, providing an expansive view of Central Park that was quite breathtaking, especially on this snowy winter's day.

As I later learned, the design concept for the duplex

was "Malibu in New York," and the apartment had been designed by the New York City architectural firm of Gwathmey Siegel and Associates. To provide an outdoor feeling, clouds against a blue background had been hand-painted on the ceiling. The furniture consisted of white canvas sofas and blue-and-gray leather armchairs framed by a variety of greenery and azaleas in baskets. Although a great deal of attention had been given to the smallest details, I found the apartment somewhat overdone and too fussy for my taste.

After I waited for approximately thirty minutes, Miss Thomas finally made her entrance in a soft pink jogging suit. My appointment had obviously been squeezed into an already busy schedule; it was swift and to the point. Miss Thomas made it quite clear that she ran the show and wanted the apartment managed to perfection. Since I had been raised with a strict, formal upbringing and had spent over half of my life in service to the rich and famous, I felt fully qualified for the job at hand.

"I expect promptness six days a week, with Sundays off," she said as she continued with the job description. "It's a busy household, and I conduct a large part of my business here." Miss Thomas warned me that even though she and Phil were the only ones in residence, the hours would be long. I assured her that I was extremely flexible and willing to put in whatever hours were required to get the job done. "Phil and I travel frequently and what we really need is someone who will run the apartment as if it were his own."

After concluding this brief introductory speech, Miss Thomas rose to give me the guided tour, whisking me from room to room on the first floor and then up to the second floor, which was made up entirely of the master suite. It contained Phil's study, a kitchenette, bedroom, bathroom, and a dressing room so large that it reminded me of Joan Crawford's dressing suite pictured in the opening sequence of *Mommie Dearest* (a prophetic thought, as it turned out). Marlo then glanced at her watch and said, "Think it over. If you want the job, you can start next Monday at 8:45 A.M. I have a meeting to attend. Billie will show you out." She glanced again at her watch and quickly left the room.

Billie escorted me to the front door and asked if compensation had been discussed. I told her the subject had not been mentioned and that I would hold to the salary requirements listed on my resumé, which I assumed Miss Thomas had reviewed. As I would later learn, Marlo always paid her staff extremely well and above the market value because she believed it necessary to pay quality people what they are worth. In this respect, she always proved to be a very generous employer.

Later that day, I went to dinner with a close friend to discuss the outcome of the meeting. After weighing the pros and cons, I decided to accept the job, concluding that it certainly could not be any worse than some of the other positions I had held. I also felt that working for people in entertainment would be more interesting than for the Park Avenue crowd who spent most of their time charity hopping. As the months went by, I realized what an understatement that assumption had been.

The next day, I telephoned Marlo's secretary and accepted the position. An assignment which surely would prove to be the greatest challenge of my career: life with "That Girl" and Phil.

210

The preceding pages comprise the opening chapter of *That Girl and Phil* (St. Martin's Press, 1990). My days working for Marlo Thomas and Phil Donahue were so filled with hilarious mishaps and unbelievable escapades I felt the experience merited an entire book of its own. When I agreed to supervise the Thomas–Donahue's New York penthouse, Connecticut country estate, forty-foot yacht, and sizable staff, I never imagined that it would prove to be the last great challenge of my career as a majordomo.

The three years I spent working for the Thomas–Donahues forced me to seriously think about changing professions. I finally realized that all the time and energy I devoted to making other peoples' lives and projects work was not benefiting my long-term future. My life was no longer my own. It really never had been, but at least it used to be a satisfying experience. This new breed of employer made it increasingly difficult to enjoy one's work. I wanted to invest my time and talents in my own projects and creative endeavors, so that in time I would have accomplished something tangible which was mine. I was fortunate that after eight long years my grandmother's estate was finally settled, enabling me to secure my financial future.

One of the reasons I had decided to write *That Girl and Phil* was to address the issue of employers who are disrespectful or abusive toward their employees. Everyone has at some point in his or her life worked for someone whom they feel has been offensive, discriminatory, or difficult.

Are we expected to constantly tolerate such treatment merely because we must work for a living? Why do individuals who are privileged enough to have fame, fortune, or positions of authority feel compelled to use their advantages as a weapon against the rest of us? And how do we defend ourselves against such employers without appearing insubordinate and risking termination? I felt it was time for someone to say "Enough!" You are paid a salary to perform your job to the best of your abilities; but that does not entitle an employer to treat you anyway he or she likes. Somehow these individuals have to be held accountable for their actions.

Once I had made the decision to commit my experiences to paper I was certain that I would never be involved in another domestic situation again. But if there is anything certain in this life, it's that it is filled with uncertainty. Just when we think we have permanently closed, locked, and nailed a door shut, it somehow unexpectedly pops open. I had one more employer to serve (albeit briefly) before I set down the serving tray and pulled out the pen.

Fifteen

One particularly humid August day in 1989, I was seated at the typewriter in my Greenwich Village apartment, compiling a list of editors and agents. My ex-wife telephoned and prefaced the conversation by stating that she had an enormous favor to ask of me. Sally was the type of individual who never took advantage of anyone: If she required my assistance I assumed it was of some importance. She began by explaining that one of her mother's friends, Mrs. Etka Schwartz, had recently lost her husband. Mrs. Schwartz was in the process of consolidating a Park Avenue penthouse and a Bridgehampton beach house into a newly purchased Fifth Avenue apartment. The widow was very scatter-brained and desperately needed someone to help organize her new life. Sally's mother had mentioned that I performed this type of work. Mrs. Schwartz felt it was a sign from her dearly departed husband; she asked if there was any possibility I could help her out for a month or two.

My ex-wife gently pleaded the case. "Desmond, be a

dear and help Etka sort things out. She'll never be able to organize the move on her own. It's the kind of job you could do with your eyes closed. Please, as a favor to me.''

It was a difficult decision. I was trying to create a new life for myself; the thought of facing packing boxes and Fifth Avenue apartments once again sent a chill through my spine. I told Sally I had retired from my career as a majordomo. Unfortunately, her mother had almost promised the desperate widow she would be able to secure my services; Sally didn't want to let her mother down. I felt pushed into a domestic corner.

My ex-wife rarely asked me for anything; if this was important to her then I should make the effort to be accommodating. After all, it would only be for a month— two at the most. How bad could it be?

A white-gloved attendant ushered me up to a Fifth Avenue duplex. As I stepped off the elevator an apartment door opened slightly, revealing a heavily mascaraed eye peering through the two-inch gap. Suddenly the door flew open; I was greeted by an anorexically thin, leathery-skinned woman dressed in a brown velveteen pantsuit. Before I had the opportunity to introduce myself, Mrs. Schwartz rather curtly informed me that I was twelve minutes early. I was not in a particularly indulgent mood. Although I felt like telling the widow her appearance was five years late, I held my tongue.

''I'm Mrs. Schwartz. You can call me Mrs. Schwartz. Come in, come in, before the neighbors see you standing there. I don't know if someone took the trouble to mention it but my husband just died. It wouldn't do for any-

214

one to see strange men arriving at my apartment in the middle of the afternoon. Hurry up! Come in!"

Mrs. Schwartz swept me into the library: a cream colored room with brown carpet, brown furniture, and shelves filled with brown books. The space was dark, cluttered, and very depressing. Imagine my surprise when she told me this was the only room in the apartment she wasn't going to touch because it was so stylish.

My potential employer poised her thin frame between two rather lumpy cushions, poured herself a martini, and began to describe what her expectations were: The list was endless. She asked me all about my previous employer—Marlo Thomas—and wanted to know what she paid. When I told her the salary, she almost choked on an olive. I quickly explained that I was basically doing this as a favor to my ex-wife; money was not an important issue.

Next came yet another tour of yet another huge and hideously designed apartment. The decor was very dated, with brown shag carpeting throughout. Mrs. Schwartz owned an extensive collection of impressionist paintings which she had temporarily hung in various spots around the rooms. It was an impressive collection. But two Monets, a Cassat, and a van Gogh all on the same wall somehow lessened the magnificence of each work of art.

Mrs. Schwartz concluded the high-speed tour by escorting me through a narrow hallway off the kitchen. She opened the door to an eight-by-ten-foot windowless room with paint peeling off the walls; the adjoining bathroom offered a cracked sink, rusty bathtub, water-stained ceiling, and a window overlooking a brown brick wall.

"You know, you can live-in if you like. All this can be yours, I don't mind. No charge. Really."

I pictured my beautiful white duplex overlooking the Hudson River and shuddered at the thought of being held prisoner in this tiny cell.

"That's very kind and generous of you, Mrs. Schwartz, but I have an apartment of my own I'm quite happy with."

When she frowned with disappointment at my response, I thought her face resembled a pleated skirt. I'm certain she was lonely and would have welcomed the company, but there was a limit to how far I would extend myself for my ex-wife.

Mrs. Schwartz escorted me back to the foyer; against my better judgment I agreed to work for a month to get her settled into her new home.

Although Mrs. Schwartz had inherited a fortune and owned a multi-million dollar art collection, she was ruthless when it came to minimizing household expenditures. She insisted on doing all of the grocery shopping herself and asked me to give her a list of whatever I required each day. She loved to dress in one of her expensive outfits and venture out onto the streets of New York with Matisse—an extremely vocal Maltese which she carried in a large Fendi handbag. Mrs. Schwartz explained that Matisse loved the fresh air but hated to walk. I was busy organizing construction workers, electricians, and decorators; her absence from the apartment each morning made my life easier.

On the third day of the job I was meeting with a representative from The Museum of Modern Art to discuss the best way to restore a Picasso. Mrs. Schwartz dashed into the library where we were seated. I stared in disbelief at a sixty-eight-year-old woman dressed in an orange and yellow leather jacket with matching mini skirt. She wobbled on two-inch heels, presumably trying to balance her enormous wide-brimmed hat. I knew she was ready to go grocery shopping.

Mrs. Schwartz stated that she had to speak with me about an extremely urgent matter. I excused myself and followed her into the kitchen.

"Desmond, I just can't believe this!" she exclaimed, slapping the shopping list against the refrigerator as if it was a fly-swatter.

"Is there a problem with my handwriting?" I asked.

"Eight rolls of paper towels and another jar of marmalade! How is it possible! Do you know how much a roll of paper towels costs? A dollar twenty-nine! And that's if I walk the extra four blocks to Gristede's!" She shook the list with such force her Chanel bracelets clattered. "At this rate I'll spend a hundred dollars this month on paper alone! I'm a widow. I can't afford such extravagances. What is happening to our supplies?!"

I paused for a moment, expecting Allen Funt to pop out of one of the closets and scream, "Smile, you're on 'Fifth Avenue' camera!" The only popping in the room, however, came from Mrs. Schwartz's overly made-up eyes. I couldn't believe she was serious. Standing before me was a woman wearing $10,000 worth of clothes and jewelry, and she was in a state about less than $20 worth of groceries.

"Well, what explanations do you have to offer!" she demanded.

I was losing my patience as rapidly as the mini'd matron was losing her dignity.

"Mrs. Schwartz," I began. "We are in the early process of renovating your apartment. Plaster dust is everywhere, which requires daily cleaning. I'm certain you would agree that the modest investment in cleaning supplies is preferable to living in the midst of dirt and dust. As to the jam—I use several spoonfuls on my scones when I take tea at three-thirty P.M. Is that going to be a problem?"

Mrs. Schwartz' black Crayola eyebrows began erratically twitching like the graph on a lie detector. "Perhaps you could make an effort to utilize one teaspoon per scone. I think that's a reasonable amount."

I felt momentarily dizzy with a flashback of Gayfryd Steinberg's "one yogurt per day" quota for the maids. Suddenly I pictured Mrs. Schwartz measuring the side of a jar of Sorrel Ridge Orange Marmalade each day.

"About this paper towel crisis, I'll have to give it some more thought. I'm going shopping now." She pivoted, almost sliding off her heels into the sink. At the last moment she caught her balance and wobbled out the door.

There have been very few moments in my life which I have found shocking, but this was definitely one of them. The situation was too ridiculous to even think about; I decided to get on with my work.

Two days later Mrs. Schwartz waltzed into the kitchen, her slim frame draped in what appeared to be bed linens. She looked like she was about to go to a toga party for anorexics.

"Desmond," she cried, "I've done it!"

I thought perhaps she was about to tell me she had just

218

pledged with a sorority for senior citizens and this was part of some bizarre initiation rite.

"Done what?" I replied, picking up my cue.

"I've solved our paper towel crisis," she proudly announced. To celebrate her triumph she began sailing through the kitchen like Isadora Duncan in an improvisational moment.

I have been around rich and eccentric people all of my life. I thought she was draped in the bed sheets to amuse herself. I never made a connection between her costume and the resolution of her crisis. Mrs. Schwartz carefully unwrapped one of the sheets from around her neck and began waving it in the air like a cowboy about to lasso a mad calf.

"These sheets are the perfect solution, don't you think?! If you cut them into two-foot squares they'll make wonderful rags to clean the apartment with. They can be washed and used again the next day. Just think," she continued as she twirled around the kitchen, "I may never have to purchase paper towels again!"

I turned the corners of my lips upward, hoping my face would masquerade the sense of nausea which was sweeping up from my toes to the tip of my head. I was doing this merry widow a favor and now she was asking me to tear old bed sheets so she could save twenty dollars a week.

I told Mrs. Schwartz that her resourcefulness had left me speechless; although I would welcome the opportunity to share in her celebration and begin the creative process of transforming bed linens into rags, I felt ill and had to leave immediately.

The following Monday I telephoned my thrifty employer and regrettably informed her that I had a family emergency which required my immediate departure for England. "I'm so very sorry, Mrs. Schwartz, but in light of the circumstances I may not return for several months. I feel it is only proper that I resign. Perhaps I can recommend someone to take over my position."

Isadora Duncan suddenly transformed herself into Sarah Bernhardt. She cried, she begged, she demanded, she pleaded. But to no avail. I had made my decision.

I hung up the telephone and for the first time in years I felt as if my life were my own.

I thought about all the Christmas and Easter holidays which had been spent trying to make someone else's life special. My memory flooded with the images of castles, châteaux, villas, and yachts which, no matter how extraordinarily beautiful, were never someplace I could call home. I realized I would never have to bite my tongue in silence from a rude employer or try to organize a perfect life for anyone again.

From that moment on I began to serve myself.

Epilogue

Having survived an extremely diverse career which whisked me around the world, I presently lead a comparatively quiet life, dividing my time between New York and Connecticut, creating books and preparing lectures. In addition to my writing projects, I tour America's college campuses and civic organizations, addressing the topic of how to get along with your employer utilizing concepts of good manners and etiquette.

People frequently ask if I regret relinquishing my career as a majordomo. Although I occasionally miss certain employers and the experiences we shared, there was little doubt that I had reached the point in my life where it was time to move on. A job *must* be enjoyable; after all, we spend the majority of our waking hours at work. The pleasure and satisfaction which I once derived from serving the very rich disappeared along with the sophisticated, well-mannered employers for whom I had once worked. The type of individuals who required my services were not the sort of people I wished to associate with: arrogant, ill-mannered, self-centered socialites who felt you exchanged your rights as a human being for an agreed-upon salary.

An employer can purchase your time, but he cannot buy your respect and admiration. Respect must be earned by both parties one day at a time. Sadly, a majordomo (or any kind of domestic) is frequently looked down upon as some sort of menial servant. A domestic employee's primary goal is to improve the life of his employer. But he is not there to be exploited and/or treated in a less than humanitarian manner. A simple smile, "good morning," or a "thank you" goes a surprisingly long way. In my career I never asked anyone to do anything which I was not willing or able to do myself. I treated my staff with kindness and compassion even though I had to perform unpleasant tasks at times upon direct orders from above.

It is imperative to wake up each morning with a sense of enthusiasm and pride about your job. Being unhappy in the workplace will ultimately have a detrimental effect on your personal life. I'm certain my marriage suffered because my tenure with the Steinbergs was one of the most unpleasant, stressful periods of my career. I no longer suppress the urge to defend myself against abusive behavior, nor do I quietly tolerate demeaning insults.

As both a majordomo and an author I have tried to defend the rights of employees, sincerely believing that most people want to do a good job. Unfortunately, years of either abusive or indifferent treatment have broken the spirits and ultimately lessened the job performance of many individuals. Like a minority which quietly suffers the indignities of discrimination until it can no longer remain silent, employees must eventually find a way to speak out and say, "Enough. I demand to be treated with the same respect and consideration which you require of me." No more, no less.

The majority of my career has been extremely rewarding. I have met an amazing assortment of wild and wonderful characters, and have enjoyed an extremely privileged life available to very few. My experiences have taught me to flow with the tide and find a way to appreciate what each new day brings. I am closer to my family now and happy and grateful to be living in America.

People often ask me if there is anyone I haven't worked for that I would like to. Considering my literary efforts, I think the question is moot. But I do have great respect and admiration for Oprah Winfrey, Whoopi Goldberg, and Madonna—self-made, highly unique individuals who have worked hard to achieve their success without sacrificing their social consciousness. If one of these extremely talented women telephoned one day and asked me to organize a quiet dinner for two hundred, who knows? Life is filled with such uncertainty. If anyone had predicted ten years ago that this buoyantly British butler would become an author in his late thirties I would have laughed.

My memories are continually haunted by the image of an angelic-faced lady standing under the shade of a large oak tree in her perfectly manicured garden. Dressed in a flowery painter's smock and an enormous white picture hat, my grandmother tried to create a colorful vision of the world within the confines of a formal English estate. After almost forty years, Nansy's inspirational words still guide my life: "If you dare to be who you truly want to be, you risk enjoying every day of your life." For an eccentric ex-actress who liked a nip of sherry now and again, she was a very wise woman, indeed.

I have always dared to be who and what I wanted, making many strange and unusual diversions along the path; it's been an incredibly entertaining ride which has transported me to places about which most people can only dream. I may be judged or criticized for my choices—from planning a drag party for my sister's fifth birthday to writing books about my experiences with previous employers—but I take full responsibility for them. These specific choices have allowed me to create my own unique adventure; I wouldn't have it any other way.

Although I'm no longer a first-class, fast-paced, globe-trotting majordomo, my life is far from boring. The exotic escapades I once had in opulent palaces and desert tents now take place on the pages of books. I am extremely fortunate to have found a new career which is as potentially stimulating, creative, and entertaining as my years as a majordomo. And being spared the tedious task of constantly packing and unpacking suitcases is a most welcome relief.

As I hypnotically stare at the paper in the typewriter, watching my life unfold before my eyes, I am reminded of the final line of the Steven Sondheim and James Lapine musical *Sunday in the Park with George:*

White. A blank page or canvas. His favorite.
So many possibilities . . .

I have to agree.